Merchants of Misery

How Corporate America Profits From Poverty

WITHDRAWN

Edited by
Michael Hudson

Common Courage Press   Monroe, Maine

Library of Congress Cataloging-in-Publication Data
Merchants of misery :
how corporate America profits from poverty /
edited by Michael Hudson.
p. cm.
Includes index.
ISBN 1-56751-083-3 (lib. bdg.). -- ISBN 1-56751-082-5 (pbk.)
1. Financial services industry--United States. 2. Financial services industry--United States--Corrupt practices. 3. Poor--
United States. I. Hudson, Michael, 1961-
HG181.M46   1996
332.1'0973--dc20   96-496
CIP

Common Courage Press
Box 702
Monroe, ME 04951

207-525-0900   fax: 207-525-3068

First Printing

Contents

Part V
Shattered Dreams:
New Homes, Unhappy Homeowners

Part VI
Driven to Debt:
High-Priced Car Loans and Insurance

Part VII
No Place Like Home:
The Business of Slum Lords

Part VIII
A Few Bucks a Week:
The Rent-to-Own Industry

Preface

This country's economic system is premised on the belief that all Americans should have the opportunity to build their futures. Our national economic ideology teaches us that every man and woman can get ahead if they work hard, play by the rules, and manage their resources wisely.

This book chronicles, in gripping detail, the vast holes in the economic safety net that is supposed to protect millions of low-income, minority, elderly, and working-class Americans. Sadly, the goal of equal credit opportunity and economic self-sufficiency has not been realized in vast segments of American society. More troubling, millions of Americans are being preyed upon by unscrupulous, unethical, and often fraudulent credit predators who have emerged to fill the credit void that exists in so many American communities.

Our traditional institutions have failed us. Banks, savings and loan institutions, insurance companies, and mortgage companies have redlined, discriminated, and disinvested in poor neighborhoods and communities of color. As this book pointedly documents, the absence of traditional lending institutions creates a large market for a variety of credit sharks—pawnshops, check cashers, high-priced lenders, and bogus private post-secondary schools.

Our national economic, budget, and monetary policy is based on the assumption that economic growth, on a macro *and* micro level, comes from access to capital, credit availability, and low interest rates. Thus, we seek to reduce the budget deficit to lower interest rates. The Federal Reserve Board increases the money supply to lower interest rates. All this is supposed to lead to economic opportunity for all. However, as Michael Hudson and others make clear, the absence of balanced, responsible, and broad-minded financial institutions leads to horrendous abuse and scandal—usurious interest rates, forced foreclosures, and the confiscation of property—with the most vulnerable people in society the victims.

Merchants of Misery is an important chronicle of the dirty underside of American finance. It is a *real* look at the financial scandals that affect unsuspecting American consumers every day.

—U.S. Representative Maxine Waters
March 15, 1996

Introduction
The Poverty Industry

Michael Hudson

The rise of America's poverty industry is getting harder to miss these days. Turn on the TV, late-night or daytime. Tucked amid the ads for psychic hotlines you'll hear announcers offering "rent-to-own" TVs, stereos, dinette sets with pitches like this: "Just $8.95 a week! ... We make your dreams come true—one week at a time." Or drive down the main drag in an inner-city or a blue-collar suburb, and read the signs outside the storefront loan offices: "Bad Credit? No Credit? No Problem." If you live in a neighborhood with modest incomes or a large minority population, you might open your mailbox one day to find a loan company come-on fraught with double meaning: "The Credit You Deserve."

The poverty industry is made up of an array of businesses: pawnshops, check-cashing outlets, rent-to-own stores, finance companies, used-car dealers, high-interest mortgage lenders, trade schools for the poor and uneducated. It's growing in size and raking in dollars at a dizzying pace by targeting people on the bottom third of the economic ladder—perhaps 60 million consumers who are virtually shut out by banks and other conventional merchants. Many live below the poverty line, but many more are solidly blue-collar folks squeezed by falling wages and lousy credit records. The poverty industry fills a niche for them—at a stiff price. An affluent credit-card holder can shop around and pay as little as 6 or 8 percent annual interest to borrow money and make purchases on credit. But a sheet-metal worker with a dubious credit record may pay as much as 240 percent for a loan from a pawnbroker, 300 percent for a finance-company loan, 20 percent for a second mortgage, even *2,000 percent* for a quick "payday" loan from a check-cashing outlet.

James Baldwin said it years ago: It's expensive to be poor. It's unfair to call every merchant who markets to the poor a greedy exploiter, but it *is* safe to say these transactions usually are lousy deals for their customers. Along with sky-high prices, these consumers are often victimized by dishonest sales pitches, hidden charges, forged loan documents, heavy-handed collection tactics. Slick talk and mind-numbing paper-work make it easy to prey on the financially uninitiated. "Cash out the deal before the customer comes out from under the ether," goes a saying in the high-interest mortgage market.

There's another place you can run across the poverty industry these days: Try the stock pages of your newspaper. More and more, the merchants who profit from the disadvan-taged are owned or bankrolled by the big names of Wall Street—Ford, Citibank, NationsBank, BankAmerica, American Express, Western Union. Lesser-known Wall Street companies are also grabbing a piece of the action. Add up all the busi-nesses that bottom-feed on the "fringe economy" and you'll come up with a market of $200 billion to $300 billion a year. That may be a conservative estimate. Stock analysts estimate that used-car loans for people with shaky credit now top $50 billion a year all by themselves.

In many ways, America has two economies, one for the affluent and one for the poor and near poor, black and white, who struggle from week to week. On top of that, persisting discrimination puts minority consumers at greater risk of financial shakedowns. All this makes life increasingly difficult for families striving to do better. It weakens neighborhoods and increases the class and racial divisions that now threaten America.

Things will probably get worse before they get better.

The mainstream economy profits handsomely from the growth of the fringe economy. Big companies are fueling the expansion and "incorporation" of the poverty industry by pouring in growth capital and providing the sheen of brand-name respectability to transactions that Main Street and Wall Street once viewed with distaste. At the same time, they're employing sophisticated marketing techniques to hook people accustomed to being snubbed by banks and department stores. The poverty industry offers the illusion, at least, of acceptance into the mainstream. Along Interstate 465 outside Indianapolis, a billboard promising "Instant Auto Loans" with no credit checks was emblazoned with this motto: "We Believe In You."

For-profit trade schools use the lure of federal student loans to promise high-school dropouts a way out of dead-end jobs and overdue bills. "Do you love money?" one TV commercial asks. "The feel of it, the smell of it, the way it sounds when you crunch it up? If green is your favorite color, we have a perfect job for you. Become a bank teller and get paid to work with money. ... You'll be rolling in the dough before you know it."

***

WILMA JEAN HENDERSON walked unsteadily out of Associates Financial Services and climbed behind the wheel of her car. "I went to start the ignition and my legs went to shaking so bad. And I took a deep breath and I turned my car back off and I put my head on my steering wheel and I started to cry."

The mother of seven children and stepchildren had gone to an Associates office in Montgomery, Alabama, the month before and borrowed $2,000 to fix her '87 Blazer. It was a big company, one she thought she could trust. After all, it was owned by Ford Motor Company. When she sat down with the loan officer to close the deal, she recalled, "we really didn't talk about the loan. He was talking about he was having some trouble with his car—his car was one of those little foreign ones—at the same time saying, 'Sign this. Sign this.'" She testified later that the loan officer flipped through the papers so only the signature portion of the documents showed, and some of the numbers on one document had not been filled in until after she signed it. She didn't read anything, she said, because "I trusted him—to do right."

But when Henderson went to make her first payment, she testified later, she learned that along with the $2,000, she owed another $1,200 for "add-ons" she didn't know a thing about—three kinds of credit insurance and an auto club membership. And her interest rate was 33.99 percent.

She couldn't believe it. "My mother always taught me to be honest and to treat people the way you want them to treat you," she said. "I would never have thought that someone would do you like that. A company, you know what I'm saying?"

She sued, charging fraud and alleging that one of her signatures—on the auto club membership—had been forged. The loan officer testified he told Henderson all about the interest rate, insurance and auto club. The company also maintained that given the way its forms are computer generated, it would be impossible for a document to be partially blank and then filled in later. But in the end, Associates agreed to pay Henderson a confidential settlement. A spokesman said the lender settled because it's difficult for an out-of-state company to get a "level playing field" in an Alabama courthouse.

About the same time Wilma Jean Henderson was having her run-in, Bessie and Edmon Lee were having problems of their own with Associates a couple states away in Crescent City, Florida. The Lees weren't the kind of customers banks covet. Bessie, 58, left school after 10th grade. Her husband, Edmon, 70, had a third-grade education. They met in a migrant farm camp and settled in a house built on family land with a federal grant.

Then a TV ad for a home-improvement company caught Bessie Lee's eye. The financing for the paint job led to a series of three loans from Associates, and the Lees soon found themselves with a $35,000 mortgage on their home. On their last loan, the Lees paid $3,588 in origination fees—more than 10 percent of the total and at least five times what most borrowers would pay. They received $379 directly from the loan, but paid nearly $4,000 for credit insurance. Their interest rate: 18 percent.

The Lees couldn't keep up with their $583-a-month payment, and Associates sent the sheriff's department to evict them. "I know I had a dirty deal," Bessie Lee told a *Boston Globe* reporter in 1994. "It was dirty from jump." An Associates spokesman said it lost money on the loan and had to foreclose because the Lees wouldn't work out a payment plan. The Lees hung onto their home only after community activists arranged for them to get a new loan through Bank of Boston.

Associates and other Ford financial subsidiaries have been the targets of lawsuits involving 750,000 customers or more. But Ford is not alone. Many other big lenders have become entangled in allegations of predatory practices. In 1993, NationsBank purchased a consumer-finance company,

Chrysler First, from the auto giant Chrysler Corp. The finance company, since renamed NationsCredit, brought with it an embarrassing record of legal problems. For example, an Alabama jury hit it with a $2.15 million verdict over charges it had fleeced a couple on a home-repair loan deal. Company executives deny any pattern of wrongdoing at NationsCredit.

***

THERE ARE STILL many small-time, fly-by-night operators who target the vulnerable. But it's companies like Ford and NationsBank that are fueling the growth of America's poverty industry. You can find plenty of big names behind the shadow economy:

• Finance companies make small loans at rates reaching 30 percent or more—and as much as 300 percent in a few states. NationsBank, Ford and other major companies dominate this $100-billion-plus market (Part II).

• Pawnshops and check-cashing outlets—sometimes called "fringe banks"—are mega-growth industries. The number of pawnshops has doubled in the past decade to more than 10,000. At least five pawn chains are publicly traded. In the fall of 1995, the largest, Cash America, had 325 outlets in the U.S., 34 in the United Kingdom and 10 in Sweden. It's traded on the New York Stock Exchange and is financed by NationsBank and other banks. In the U.S., Cash America's typical loan rate hovers around 200 percent.

The number of check-cashing outlets has almost tripled since the late 1980s to an estimated 5,500. ACE Cash Express is a national chain of 630-plus outlets that's growing with backing from American Express. ACE generally charges from 3 percent to 6 percent of a check's value to turn it into cash (Part III).

• Mortgage lenders work hand-in-hand with mainstream banks to target low-income and minority homeowners for high-interest loans, home repair scams and other ripoffs. Fleet Finance, the Atlanta-based subsidiary of New England's largest bank, paid more than $120 million to settle allegations it fleeced 20,000 borrowers in Georgia. Analysts estimate the market for high-rate mortgages to disadvantaged consumers at $70 billion to $100 billion a year (Part IV).

- Home-builders and their financiers offer the American dream to people with credit histories and lower incomes that would normally disqualify them from owning brand new homes. Many developers have been accused of ripping off these consumers through poor workmanship and inflated prices. The "Homes in Sunny Florida" scam is one of the nation's most enduring con games (Part V).
- Slumlords and urban real-estate financiers bleed profits from the miseries inflicted upon low-income tenants. In New York and other big cities, a network of financiers and investors make money off a shell game of properties sold and resold at inflated prices via high-interest, short-term mortgages (Part VI).
- The market for auto loans to "high-risk" borrowers has become crowded with Wall Street companies eager to reap profits from loans with interest rates of 25 percent or more. Many dealers and lenders have been accused of targeting these customers for lemon deals, high interest rates and insurance rip-offs. An Alabama jury slapped Mercury Finance—the nation's leading financier of used-car loans for high-risk customers—with a $50 million verdict over allegations it had slipped a $1,000 hidden charge into a $3,000 car loan (Part VII).
- "Rent-to-own" stores sell TVs and furniture on weekly and monthly installment plans at prices that equal interest rates of 100, 200, even 300 percent. The number of rent-to-own stores has grown from about 2,000 to 7,500 since the early 1980s. Thorn EMI PLC—a British conglomerate that owns the Beatles' label, EMI Records—is the dominant player in the $4.5 billion a year rent-to-own market (Part VII).
- Trade schools and banks have earned billions by peddling the dream of good jobs to high-school dropouts. Many take advantage of the easy access to federal student-loan money by running or financing sham schools that do little to educate and leave students with ruined credit and big loan debts (Part IX).

***

THESE BUSINESSES are flourishing because there's money to be made in serving the downscale market. Ford's Associates Corp., which owns Associates Financial Services, has posted record profits each year for the past two decades—including $972 million before taxes in 1994. In fact, consumer-finance companies routinely earn double or triple the return on assets that banks do. Mercury Finance, the used-car financier, rang up a return on assets in 1994 of 9.4 percent—six times as much, *Forbes Magazine* notes, as what the best-run banks earn. From 1989 to 1995, Mercury's stock value climbed eight-fold.

Many credit-card companies have discovered the most profitable segment of their portfolios are "secured cards" issued to consumers with lousy credit records. Secured-card customers deposit money in a savings account and then essentially borrow it back when they use the card. The idea is that this will help them clean up their credit records and graduate to real bankcards. But they pay a high cost—application fees of $65, annual fees as high as $75, interest rates reaching 22 percent.

Secured cards first appeared in 1982, but didn't draw the attention of Citibank and other big credit-card issuers until the early 1990s. They're one of several financial wrinkles, invented or perfected in the go-go '80s, that are now driving the poverty industry. Another example: the "mortgage-backed" securities market pioneered by Wall Street's Salomon Brothers. These securities are legitimate investment products that have actually helped nudge down mortgage rates, even for credit-impaired borrowers. But their creation also opened a vast pool of money for shady lenders.

Here's how it works: First, a scam lender uses high-pressure tactics to make loans at huge rates to the financially desperate. Then the lender sells the mortgages—that is, the right to collect the debt—to a larger lender. In turn, the bigger player sells securities backed by the income stream from pools of these loans. The smaller operators walk away with a wad of cash that bankrolls still more predatory loans. Investors get low risk and high returns. If borrowers complain their loans were tainted by fraud, investors insulate themselves from legal claims by blaming it on the original lender.

In the early 1990s Fleet Finance used mortgage-backed securities to help ring up profits of $50 million a year from loans to borrowers shunned by mainstream banks. That cash flow gave Providence-based Fleet Bank the clout it needed to buy the Bank of New England and make it the region's largest bank.

In its wake Fleet left people like Annie Diggs. Like many of Fleet's victims, she was poor, black, elderly, a widow. Diggs was born in Macon, Georgia in 1915, a few months after her father drowned. She was raised on a farm by a great aunt until boll weevils invaded. Diggs married at 14 and had 10 children. She was a maid at a funeral home for the last 27 years of her work life. Since retiring, her only income had been her late husband's $515-a-month railroad pension plus $60 a month in food stamps.

Diggs had lived in the same house on Blakley Street in Augusta, Georgia, for half a century. In 1987, her roof was leaking and she went to a bank to borrow for repairs. She owed a balance of just $343 on her mortgage, but the bank turned her away. Later she got a call from a loan company that promised to arrange the repairs for $3,300. She says the manager talked her into borrowing a bit more so she could pay other bills and buy a washer-dryer. Diggs signed a stack of papers she didn't understand, and ended up with a $15,000 mortgage on her house—at 18.9 percent. The lender charged her $2,595 in fees—and claimed she got $4,328 she swore she never saw.

Her roof kept leaking, her ceiling caved in. When she found out her loan had been sold to Fleet Finance, she called and complained about the shoddy work. "They said that was my problem. All they was interested in was getting the monthly payment on time." The $251 a month was almost half her income. She was on the verge of losing her home until a consumer attorney took up her cause. "I go to bed at night and get up in the morning looking for the mailman thinking I'm going to get a letter telling me to move," she told a Congressional panel. "Every time I turn around, they badger me and badger me. They won't give you a chance."

***

CREDIT ABUSES against poor and minority Americans are nothing new. The company store in mill towns and coal

camps often ensnared workers in never-ending debt. In the
Deep South before the Civil Rights Movement, many black
sharecroppers were trapped in "debt peonage"—chained to
their land after mortgaging their property and crops to
planters who advanced them money at painful rates.

Small-loan companies began popping up after the Civil
War and were everywhere by the turn of the century. Their
high interest rates—120 percent was typical—and hard-
knocks collection tactics began to draw scorn. In 1904 the *New
York Times* told of a man who lost all his furniture after borrowing $25 ("Took Even Baby's Cradle," the *Times* said). In
1913 Daniel H. Tolman, who ran small-loan companies in 63
cities, was carted away to jail for six months. The charge:
usury. "You are one of the most contemptible usurers in your
unspeakable business," the judge scolded. "The poor people
must be protected from such sharks as you. ... Men of your
type are a curse to the community, and the money they gain is
blood money." Such abuses led many states to pass laws in the
1920s and 1930s to regulate small-loan companies.

After the riots of the 1960s, the National Advisory
Commission on Civil Disorders reported that many ghetto
merchants engaged "in various exploitive tactics"—high-pressure salesmanship, bait-and-switch advertising, selling used
goods as new, charging exorbitant prices. Those sorts of complaints led to federal laws, passed in the 1960s and 1970s, that
require honest disclosures of rates and forbid deceptive practices.

But the clock is spinning backward—the dawn of the next
century looks more and more like the beginning of this one.
Many state usury laws have been watered down or erased,
and new types of transactions that skirt credit laws—such as
"rent-to-own" plans—have been invented. In a growing number of states, what once was called usury has been given a legislative stamp of approval. At least 11 of the 13 southern states
allow pawnshops to charge 240 percent on loans; Georgia
allows 300 percent.

Along with their winning lobbying efforts, high-priced
lenders have shrewdly remade their images. In the 1960s, the
consumer-finance industry's trade association began going

into schools with "education materials" touting its members' worth. It also created a Foundation for Economic Education of the Clergy, because its members were worried about ministers condemning debt from the pulpits. "When the ministers stopped telling the people that credit was a sin," a former executive with the trade group recalled, "they began to realize that this really was a way of life."

Credit *has* become a way of life. Even as a "pay-as-you-go" philosophy that condemns government debt has gained the high ground in American politics, lenders have won people over to a "get-it-now" philosophy in their personal lives.

Why wait? People who need their tax refunds right away can take out "refund-anticipation loans" through H & R Block and other tax preparers. The interest bite for getting your money a few weeks sooner is harsh—usually between 50 percent and 200 percent. That's prompted complaints these lenders take advantage of vulnerable consumers. In 1992, New York City's consumer-affairs agency accused Beneficial Corp., the leader in the refund-loan market, of misleading customers. The agency said Beneficial was disclosing a 6 percent rate on loans that actually carried annual interest rates of 225 percent. Beneficial agreed to start disclosing the true annual rate.

It's not just speed that's important to borrowers. TV commercials slyly suggest—even as they deny it—that having a credit card can make you happier, smarter, better looking. A "gold card" gives you membership in an exclusive club. Once, when you borrowed money, you called it "debt"—you owed, you were in the hole. Now it's "credit"—an admirable status conferred upon the borrower. It's a semantic trap door. "The debtor, he doesn't have credit. He's got a debt," Atlanta consumer attorney Sidney Moore says. "It's like calling the horse mackerel a tuna fish. You make something acceptable by changing its name."

Of course, if you're creating an exclusive club, somebody has to be left out. Usually, it's poor and minority consumers. The lack of banks and major supermarkets in low-income neighborhoods is an obvious example of how some consumers are locked out of the mainstream. Race-based discrimination is another. Studies across the nation have documented that banks are 60 percent to 300 percent more likely to deny mort-gages to minority applicants than white ones, even when their incomes are the same. In fact, many show *upper-income* blacks are more likely to be turned down than *lower-income* whites. A 1992 study by the Federal Reserve Bank of Boston found that even when factors such as employment history and credit records are taken into account, minorities are still more likely to be rejected. White loan officers appear more willing to over-look flaws on loan applications of borrowers who look more like them.

In 1991, a *Harvard Law Review* study of 90 Chicago car dealers revealed that white women and blacks were charged much higher prices than white men. The study used paired testers who fit middle-class profiles and employed a uniform bargaining strategy. But it still found huge disparities. White females paid markups 40 percent higher; black males paid double; black females paid triple. The study's author surmised that sales people believed blacks and women were more like-ly to be "sucker sales"—less-skillful negotiators who will pay high markups. Their final offers to black women averaged $855 more than the prices quoted to white men.

***

DEBORAH JAMES shushed her baby as he cried and wriggled in her arms. She was worried. She was in debt and couldn't see a way out.

"Stop Adrian," she told her son as he tried to get down on the floor. "Quit, quit, get up."

Across the table, a loan officer from ITT Financial Services was oozing concern—all recorded on tape and later transcribed by ITT.

"He's just tired, that is what his problem is," the loan offi-cer said. "I'll get you out of here buddy, just give me a little time. He can smile, give me a smile."

He pushed some papers in front of James.

"Look at that. OK, then this one right here. And this one right there. And this one right there."

She signed a few more documents, and it was over.

"If you've got any problems at all, don't hesitate to call me," he said. "I'll give you my card, so don't get behind that

8-ball anymore. You can always call me and I am sure that we got a solution."

Deborah James thought ITT was helping her dig out of debt. She was wrong. It was digging her deeper. Her problems began with a $300 bill at a waterbed store that ended up in the hands of ITT's Jacksonville, Florida, office. From there, ITT persuaded her to refinance her loan five times over two years—and ratcheted her debt up to more than $4,000.

In all, ITT actually loaned James $2,669. She paid back all but $45 of that in monthly installments. But her debt kept growing. Why? Because of the loans' high interest rates—between 21 percent and 30 percent—and the fees and insurance the company tacked on each time it rewrote her contract. ITT charged James more than $1,600 for credit insurance, an item consumer advocates say is virtually worthless to borrowers but produces huge profits for lenders who target the disadvantaged. The Consumer Federation of America estimates borrowers have been overcharged $500 million to $1 billion a year for credit insurance.

James never questioned the insurance; She thought it was a regular part of the loan. Like many borrowers, she trusted the lender to look out for her. At the same time, her financial desperation made her drop her guard.

People of all races and incomes make mistakes with their money. But poor and blue-collar folks are often more vulnerable. They usually have fewer choices in the marketplace, less experience with money and less education. A 1993 federal study concluded that more than one-fifth of adults—40 to 44 million people—have trouble performing simple math or reading tasks. Even educated consumers have trouble understanding the swamp of numbers—annual percentage rates, pre-paid finance charges, etc.—that accompany loan applications.

At the same time, many of these consumers are tired of being snubbed by mainstream merchants. And they're leery of the down-and-dirty images of pawnshops and inner-city retailers. All this may make them more susceptible to businesses that offer well-scrubbed images and friendly faces behind the counter. Rent-A-Center, the rent-to-own chain, claims an almost familial relationship with its customers. "Rent-A-Center is a very good friend of mine," a smiling customer in one TV commercial says. "No matter what I do," another says, "they still take me back."

Having money in our pockets, psychotherapist Arlene Modica Matthews writes, can spark feelings of warmth, sexual power, invulnerability. Not having it can produce feelings of emptiness, abandonment, anger. A Gallup poll found women with household incomes under $20,000 were more likely to be depressed than women in households earning over $50,000. This comes against a national political backdrop in which the poor are increasingly blamed for their own problems—and, it seems, for just about everybody else's problems too. Many poor people believe this themselves. A 1995 Louis Harris poll found poor Americans were more likely to believe their financial situations reflect God's regard for them.

Skillful marketers can easily find people who are in financial distress and then tap into their uncertainty and panic. Many high-interest lenders hook customers with come-ons for "debt-consolidation" loans that will stave off other creditors ("Make your bills disappear!"), or, as in the case of Deborah James and ITT, a refinancing of an existing loan that will set things straight.

There's always somebody willing to lend a hand. Not long ago, Mallory Hughes received a personalized mailing at his home in Florida from Oral Roberts. The evangelist told him it was time "to get out from under a load of debt, that financial bondage that ... makes you feel like you have nowhere to turn." Roberts' solution? Hughes should send a $100 gift to Roberts himself, so the preacher could talk with God and help Hughes begin "the war on your debt."

Hughes was upset. How could Oral Roberts know he had money problems? Jeffrey Rothfeder's book, *Privacy For Sale*, tells how: The evangelist had bought Hughes' name from one of dozens of national databanks that list suspected "deadbeats," such as people who've been turned down for credit cards or have overdue balances on their current cards. Hughes didn't bite, but doubtless many others did. These same databanks are available to any business that wants a list of people who are grasping for a way out of the money pit.

***

IN THE SPRING OF 1995, a customer walked into one of Tulsa, Oklahoma's many storefront finance companies to make a payment on her "signature loan."

The clerk didn't want her to pay down her loan. He wanted her to borrow more money. "Sure you don't want 19 dollars and 4 cents?" he asked.

"Yeah," she said.

"You sure? Keep your money and I'll give you 19.04."

"That's OK."

"Are you sure? Might not be there next time."

"I know."

She tried to walk out the door, but the loan officer wasn't giving up.

"You want 40 dollars? I'll give you 40 dollars right now. Huh?"

"No. That's OK."

"Forty dollars! I'll give it to you right now."

"For what?"

"Just cause," he said. "I'll give you 40 dollars."

"I'll manage," she said.

What the loan officer didn't know was that this scene was being recorded by a hidden camera from a local news show. KOTV's investigation revealed that finance companies in Oklahoma frequently pressure their customers to refinance. "My job was to keep everyone in debt," a former loan clerk told reporter Brett Shipp. "... We didn't tell 'em that you're going to be in debt to us for the rest of your life."

These borrowers pay eye-popping prices. Oklahoma's small-loan statute allows interest rates as high as 339 percent. A customer who borrows $90 for three months pays $42 in interest—which works out to an annual rate of 207 percent. A credit-card holder who borrows $90 at 17 percent pays about $5 in interest over the same time.

Most of Tulsa's finance companies are owned by out-of-state corporations. Tony Gentry of Royal Management in San Antonio operates 100 small-loan companies in 14 states—including five that sit side-by-side in a single block in Tulsa.

Like others in the business, he denies finance companies take advantage of their customers. "These people are smart enough to make their own decisions," he said. "They know exactly what they're doing."

But Shipp found many customers didn't realize that by refinancing, they were losing what they'd already paid on their loans and getting hit with new fees. One recalled: "I called my friend who had worked at the company and said: 'What did I just do?' And she explained to me: 'That payment you had made—you just lost. You're right back to where you started from.' Owing $132."

The loan companies also apply pressure at the back-end for the deal—to make sure they get paid. "I had to call you at home, work, mom, dad," an ex-clerk recalled. "They called people in the hospital. You could be dyin' and they would still have to call you."

Community activists are pushing for reform, but so far Oklahoma's legislators don't see the need. "I do not believe that we as government can always save people from themselves," said Sen. Dick Wilkerson, a key committee chairman. "... I believe that the purpose of all loan companies is like any other business—and that's to make money. As long as it's done within the law."

***

BUT THAT'S the problem: Too often the law allows lenders to charge outrageous rates. There's nothing wrong with charging more to cover the pitfalls of lending to people with unstable incomes or bad credit records. But most of the time the prices these consumers pay far exceed the true risks. Given reasonable rates, the vast majority will pay their bills. In fact, a 1992 study by Mortgage Insurance Companies of America found wealthier borrowers were the worst credit risks. Borrowers with mortgages of $200,000 or more were more likely to default than the average homeowner. People with homes worth less than $50,000 were better than average in paying their loans.

Race and poverty often become excuses for gouging. It doesn't make sense to say, in effect: "These customers can't really afford this. So we'll cover our risk by charging them twice as much and make it twice as hard for them to repay." Eventually you shove people over the edge, and "high-risk" becomes a self-fulfilling prophecy. ITT Financial Services' parent sold it off in pieces after at least 100,000 of its customers declared bankruptcy. Lawsuits across the nation—which eventually cost ITT more than $80 million in settlements—alleged that ITT loan officers pushed borrowers to ruin by aggressively packing credit insurance onto loans and refinancing loan contracts to pump up their debts.

Philip White, a former loan officer and assistant manager for Associates Financial Services in Alabama, says that's how the finance-company game is played—by milking as much money as possible out of customers who can't afford it. It's a high-wire act: When the game's played well, the lenders squeeze customers to the limit, and keep them there. But they can't go so far as to drive customers away, or at least not into bankruptcy.

"They skin you," White says, but "leave a little bit of skin" so they can come back later. "And skin you again."

Part I
The Geography of Discrimination:
Banking, Race and Redlining

The poverty industry begins at the bank door, where poor and minority consumers are frequently shut out of mainstream credit and services. Banks create a vacuum by closing branches and refusing loans in disadvantaged neighborhoods. Into that void come check cashers, high-rate mortgage companies and others eager to serve the bankless.

Discrimination takes many forms, often subtle, and one form can exacerbate the other. The home-mortgage market is skewed not just by loan officers' hidden racial preconceptions, but also by the biases of home-insurance companies and appraisers who are vital to the process. Joseph Boyce, a black editor at the Wall Street Journal, wrote in 1992 about trying to sell his house in Atlanta. When white appraisers came in, Boyce's family was present. The appraisers put the value of the house at just over $70,000. Before a second set of appraisers came in, Boyce removed all his family photos and had his secretary and her son, who are white, be there instead of his own family. The second time around, the house appraised $12,500 higher.

The New Redlining

It's different from the old, but minorities are still getting shortchanged

Penny Loeb, Warren Cohen and Constance Johnson,
with Joseph P. Shapiro, Kukula Glastris,
Pamela Sherrid and Andrea Wright,

U.S. News & World Report, April 17, 1995

Above the blighted neighborhood of North Philadelphia in Germantown, George and LaVerne Butts purchased an abandoned house seven years ago. It was something of a beachhead. Banks weren't making loans in the North Philadelphia area, but the Buttses persuaded them to try. They had the law on their side. The law was called the Community Reinvestment Act. Passed in 1977, the CRA requires banks to meet the credit needs of their entire communities—rich or poor, white or black. The law permits citizens to protest a bank's community lending record and win agreements for more loans. That's what the Buttses did. And thanks to their efforts, some 200 abandoned houses nearby are home now to families. Children play in the yards. The mortgages get paid on time.

But the 18-year-old act has also generated plenty of controversy. Republicans have introduced bills in the House and Senate that would exempt nearly 88 percent of the nation's banks from the CRA. Supported by banking groups, GOP leaders say the private sector is doing everything it can to make mortgage money available to lower-income Americans. The Clinton administration says more needs to be done. It is pushing for stronger CRA regulations. In the meantime, the Justice Department is taking the lead on fair lending. Two weeks ago, Justice joined a discrimination case against American Family Mutual Insurance Co. in Milwaukee. The insurer quickly agreed to settle. It will invest $14.5 million in the inner city. Says Deval Patrick, assistant attorney general for civil rights: "Our cases illustrate that there is a far greater chance that minorities will face outright denial of financing—or denial of financing at competitive rates—than will white applicants with virtually identical qualifications."

Few people dispute that federal fair-lending laws have had a positive impact on bank lending to the poor. But critics contend the lender could be doing a lot more. They concede that blatant discrimination—in which financial institutions literally drew a red line around entire neighborhoods deemed off-limits for loans and homeowner's insurance—is rare today. But formal redlining, they argue, has given way to other practices that effectively impede lending to poor neighborhoods. Compounding the problem, banks have been closing branch offices, pulling up a crucial financial anchor of many communities.

In a six-month investigation, *U.S. News* examined banking, lending and home-insurance coverage in poor and minority communities. The inquiry was based on an unprecedented study of nine sets of banking and insurance industry data, including more than 24 million mortgage records. More than 200 interviews were conducted in 12 cities. These are the principal findings of the inquiry:

• The number of poor and minority homeowners who cannot obtain full-coverage property insurance is nearly 50 percent greater than that for residents of mostly white, middle-class areas. Poor Americans also pay more than twice, on average, what residents of middle-class neighborhoods pay for property insurance. In high-minority, low-income areas, residents pay an average of $7.21 per $1,000 of homeowner's insurance. Residents of low-minority, middle-income neighborhoods, by contrast, pay an average of $3.53 per $1,000. Insurance carriers' loss costs are demonstrably higher for urban areas—accounting for more stringent underwriting rules and higher premiums. Even so, a study done last year by the National Association of Insurance Commissioners reviewed three decades of insurance industry performance in urban areas and concluded: "Insurance redlining is widespread and has adversely affected residents of poor and minority neighborhoods." On current conditions, the study was less definitive. Higher prices and lack of insurance availability in poor, urban neighborhoods, it found, "may be driven, at least in part, by incorrect assumptions about the risk characteristics" of those neighborhoods.

• Despite federal laws that encourage banks to lend to the communities they serve, banks are fleeing poor neighborhoods in ever greater numbers. An examination of Federal Deposit Insurance Corp. data for 12 major cities representing 31 percent of the nation's urban population found that in the past two decades, the number of bank branches in white neighborhoods had tripled compared with the number of bank branches in mostly minority areas. Nationally, according to the *U.S. News* study, there are an average of 38 bank branches per 100,000 residents in white areas but only 22 branches in minority neighborhoods. Two decades ago, the numbers were roughly equal. They have become unbalanced in recent years as banks have closed branches in poor areas.

• Federal laws make it a crime to discriminate against mortgage applicants seeking to buy homes in mostly minority areas. But the *U.S. News* survey found that middle-income black applicants from mostly minority areas were more than twice likely to be rejected for mortgage loans as middle-income whites living in mostly white areas. For blacks, the rejection rate was 37 percent; for whites, it was just 18 percent. Overall, residents of middle-income white neighborhoods received 61 percent more mortgage loans than residents of middle-income minority areas did.

The bottom line

Bankers and insurance executives say they work hard to do more business in poor and minority neighborhoods, and many do, particularly through community development banks. But higher crime rates and tumbling property values make lending in poor areas difficult. "Banks *want* to make loans," says the American Bankers Association's James McLaughlin. "It's how they make their money. ... The bottom line is that they're in the business of making loans." Leo Jordan, a vice president with State Farm Insurance Co., agrees. "There really isn't evidence of intentional discrimination by insurers against urban residents," he says. "What you have are neutral underwriting rules that have a disproportionate impact upon minority, urban residents."

Obtaining full-coverage insurance for a home is nearly as important as finding the financing to buy one. In Toledo, Ohio,

Deborah Quinn-Lucy, a black high school teacher, owns a handsome frame house in a neighborhood of mostly well-maintained homes. The neighborhood is in central Toledo. Most of the residents are black. In the past four years, Quinn-Lucy has had her homeowner's insurance canceled twice. The reasons have differed each time. One insurer claimed that her house is located in front of an alley, creating a security problem. Another canceled over a broken window that actually was being replaced.

The crime rate in Quinn-Lucy's neighborhood is significantly higher than that in nearby Maumee. In 1993, the city of Toledo reported 64 property crimes for every 1,000 residents. In Maumee, the rate was 40.5 crimes per 1,000. The numbers mirror the national averages almost exactly: In central cities of 1 million people or more, the national average is 65 burglaries per 1,000 households, compared with 45 per 1,000 households in suburban areas.

Less costs

The numbers are instructive on two levels. First, while the crime rate in inner cities is higher than in the suburbs, it is not *twice* as high, as is the average insurance premium paid by inner-city residents. Second, insurance carriers clearly have greater loss costs on policies sold in inner cities, but except for the most blighted inner cities, crime stats don't appear to justify decisions to exclude entire neighborhoods from insurance coverage. State Farm Insurance Co. is currently under investigation for its sales practices in Quinn-Lucy's neighborhood in Toledo and in several other Ohio cities. State Farm says it has broken no laws and is cooperating with the inquiry.

Insurers say they do not discriminate against residents of poor and minority neighborhoods. Rather, they say, their decisions on where and what kinds of insurance to sell are dictated by business reasons. One key factor is property values. In many inner-city neighborhoods, the value of housing stock of all kinds has fallen in recent years. That makes it difficult or impossible to offer "replacement value" coverage—policies that pay to rebuild a structure and replace its furnishings at today's costs.

Still, a growing number of policy cancellations have

attracted the attention of federal regulators. Although it has no statutory authority to police insurance carriers, the federal government can take action if there is the suspicion of civil rights violations. That is the authority the Department of Housing and Urban Development cited in opening its investigation of State Farm's sale practices in Ohio. HUD is also examining Allstate's sales of homeowner's policies in Illinois and those of Nationwide Insurance Enterprise in Louisville, Atlanta, Milwaukee and Chicago. A spokesperson for Allstate says the company is in compliance with the law and is cooperating with the government inquiries. Nationwide has informed HUD that it has no authority to investigate the company. A spokesperson says the company's sales policies comply with all applicable laws.

Wide gap

In its study of the insurance industry's performance in urban areas, the National Association of Insurance Commissioners collected data on the cost and type of policies sold in 33 metropolitan areas in 20 states. The study is considered the most comprehensive ever done on the subject. After statistically ruling out other factors, the NAIC study found that only 57.6 percent of the houses in high-minority, low-income areas were insured at all, compared with 81.5 percent in white, high-income areas.

In a controversial settlement with Maryland-based Chevy Chase Federal Savings Bank last year, the Justice Department cited evidence of discriminatory lending practices. Chevy Chase had a policy of opening branches only in mostly white neighborhoods, where it intended to sell mortgages, Justice said. In its settlement, Chevy Chase admitted no wrongdoing but agreed to open three new branches in mostly black neighborhoods and make $7 million available in nonconventional mortgage loans.

Chevy Chase was unusual. In other cities, despite fair-lending laws like the CRA, which is supposed to penalize banks for failing to serve people in all parts of their service areas, banks regularly ignore or underserve inner-city neighborhoods. The Dime Savings Bank of New York, for example, said it serves New York, except the Bronx, suburban Long

Island, affluent Westchester County and areas upstate including Albany and Buffalo. "The Dime's communities consist of neighborhoods that are home to people of diverse ethnic and socioeconomic backgrounds," the bank's brochure stated. "We delineate our CRA communities by incorporating neighborhoods, including low- and moderate-income areas, located around our branch offices."

But the bank's map of its service area omitted the entire area of Harlem north of 117th Street—despite the fact that the area is part of New York. Last year, Dime agreed to include the rest of Harlem in maps of its service area. After a challenge by a Bronx community group threatened to scuttle Dime's application to merge with the Anchor Savings Bank, it added the Bronx. A spokesperson says Dime made the decision earlier but hadn't published it.

The loss of bank branches creates a Catch-22 situation. Banks typically lend in their service areas, most often defined as areas around their branches. Fewer branches means fewer loans. In the 12 cities analyzed by *U.S. News*, the number of banks per 100,000 residents in minority and white areas was roughly equal in 1970. By 1993, the most recent year for which records are available, there were three times as many banks per 100,000 residents of white areas as there were for every 100,000 residents of minority areas.

Baltimore was one of the cities most affected by bank flight from poor areas. In 1970, the number of banks serving the city's white and minority neighborhoods was nearly even. By 1993, minority areas had just one bank branch for every five located in white neighborhoods. For Mary Harden, the nearest bank now is a 20-minute bus ride away. Like a lot of her neighbors, Harden goes to a commercial check casher now—paying a fee of several dollars each time.

The stories differ, but not much. Not too long ago, Chandra Ward wanted to buy a house. At $15,000, the place was a steal, well within her budget. A single black woman with a steady job working for Federal Express, Ward saw her mortgage loan application rejected almost immediately—the little bungalow was in a mostly black neighborhood in central Memphis. When Ward tried to buy a second house, her loan application for $71,500 sailed right through. The second house was in a racially mixed area.

The *U.S. News* analysis found that differences in mortgage-lending rates between whites and minorities could not be accounted for fully by income levels. In white areas where household incomes were at least as much as the area median, as determined by HUD, there were an average of 45 mortgage loans per 1,000 houses. In minority areas at the same income level, there were just 28 loans per 1,000 houses.

Assessing such disparities is tricky. Many residents of poor and minority neighborhoods don't believe they can qualify for mortgage loans and so don't apply. An inability to secure full-coverage homeowner's insurance further complicates the picture, as does the secondary market for conventional mortgages. Many big lenders sell the home loans they make to buyers like the Federal National Mortgage Association. Secondary-market buyers have strict criteria: Buyers must either have made a down payment on the home of at least 20 percent of the purchase price or they must buy private mortgage insurance, which guarantees repayment of the loan if the homeowner defaults. Many poor people cannot come up with a 20 percent down payment. Many cannot qualify for or afford private mortgage insurance.

The disparities in mortgage lending by neighborhood are important. The CRA was passed as a key element of the 1977 Housing and Urban Development Act, whose stated purpose was to outlaw "redlining"—defined as a refusal by a financial institution to make mortgage loans to certain neighborhoods because of their racial composition, income level of the residents or age of the housing stock. The *U.S. News* findings for middle-income black and white mortgage applicants are best understood not by the race of the applicant but by the *racial composition* of the neighborhoods in which loan applicants sought to purchase homes. Jonathan Fiechter, acting director of the U.S. Office of Thrift Supervision, one of four federal agencies responsible for enforcing fair-lending laws, calls the trend dismaying. "I don't think we have the blatant discrimination we had in the 1950s and 1960s," Fiechter says. "I think it tends to be more unintentional, which may be just as egregious in some sense."

That's why the stakes in the current fight over the CRA

are so high, its supporters say—arguing that the act is a linch-pin in the federal anti-discrimination enforcement machine, a "trigger" that can bring other anti-bias laws to bear.

Everyone seems to have a gripe about the law. Critics call CRA rules burdensome; others say the law has been ineffective in promoting far greater levels of lending to minorities.

Both, in a way, are right. The American Bankers Association's McLaughlin says banks spend $12 billion annually trying to comply with the CRA—and most of that goes for paperwork—an expensive and time-consuming burden. "There are some real small banks in this country that only have seven, eight employees that have to have 15 or 16 different written policies. ... It doesn't make a lot of sense."

Challenges generate loans.

The law *has* done some good. Under the CRA, challenges to banks have resulted in pledges of more than $30 billion in loans to minority neighborhoods nationwide. In Illinois, Harris Bank, Northern Trust Bank and First National Bank of Chicago promised to lend $153 million over five years to poor neighborhoods. An evaluation found that the program had generated $117.5 million in new loans by the start of the fifth year—and almost no direct loan losses.

But other evidence supports the argument that the CRA is a weak tool at best. Prior to 1992, the four bank regulatory agencies responsible for enforcement of fair-lending laws referred potential violators to the Department of Justice just one time; no enforcement action resulted. In the past two years, there have been 16 bank referrals to the Justice Department for racial and ethnic discrimination. Two lawsuits were filed as a result of those referrals. The Justice Department sent 11 of the complaints back to the agencies that originated them, citing insufficient evidence of violations or recommending administrative enforcement. Three referrals are under investigation.

One big reason for the complaints about the CRA is the approach the law takes toward enforcement. Many who supported passage of the law initially said that banks ought to be made to serve all areas of the communities in which they did business. In exchange for government services like federal deposit insurance, the theory went, banks should have to meet certain minimal lending standards. Lawmakers wanted performance. What they didn't want was an overly rigid regulatory tool. What they got was a law that barely quantified lending activity at all.

Ratings

Federal bank regulators are supposed to evaluate lending records every other year. Banks are rated on 12 factors. Only three have anything to do with where loans are actually made and whether banks locate branches in poor neighborhoods. Three other rating factors relate only to paperwork. Banks are thus assessed, for example, on the quality of brochures they publish about their lending philosophy. Eugene Ludwig, comptroller of the currency, concedes the point: "What the law asks us to evaluate is 'Are you meeting with the community? Are you advertising to the community?'"

Even defenders of the CRA call the rating system inadequate. Banks can be given one of four grades. In 1994, fewer than 1 percent of all banks—the exact figure is 0.3 percent, just 17 banks out of 5,592 examined—received a lowest CRA grade, a term regulators call substantial noncompliance. Of the 100 banks that ranked lowest in a separate *U.S. News* review of mortgage loans to minorities, not a single bank received the noncompliant grade.

Seeking favor

The *U.S. News* review also found extraordinary variation in the kind of information banks provide to regulators. One bank asked the FDIC for a favorable CRA rating because some of its employees participated in a community window-washing project; the FDIC approved the request. Another bank asked the Federal Reserve for a high CRA rating, in part because it established a $60,000 line of credit for local businesses to purchase Girl Scout Cookies. The Fed commended the bank for the effort.

William Proxmire, the former chairman of the Senate Banking Committee who authored the CRA, envisioned regulators stepping in to block mergers and acquisitions because of poor CRA ratings. In fact, federal regulators have blocked almost no applications for mergers and acquisitions because of poor CRA grades. Since 1977, according to banking consultant Kenneth Thomas, regulators have denied just 20 of more than 77,000 applications for adding branches or merging with other banks.

Community groups say this is a critical time for the nation's inner cities. With interest rates higher than they were a year ago, borrowing is more expensive for most Americans. In the nation's poorest neighborhoods, the problems and difficulties are worse.

While the 104th Congress decides what to do now about the Community Reinvestment Act, banks and their Washington supporters are anxious to make their case. They are likely to get a sympathetic hearing. In the 1993-94 election cycle, banks and mortgage companies made nearly $12 million in campaign contributions. One of every five dollars went to key members of the banking committees.

Part II
Small Loans, Big Profits:
The Finance Company Business

Consumer-finance companies are lenders of last resort for people with modest incomes or bad credit, or for consumers who need money faster than banks can respond. They came into being to make small loans that weren't secured by real estate, but now many offer mortgages in addition to personal loans.

They charge high interest rates—typically from 20 to 40 percent on smaller debts—but most make a big slice of their profits by selling credit insurance with their loans. Credit insurance is supposed to cover the debt if borrowers get sick, lose their jobs or die. It's a good idea for some, but too often it's an overpriced bit of padding foisted on the unsuspecting. The Consumer Federation of America has called it "the nation's worst insurance rip-off." While other types of life insurance typically pay out 70 cents or more in claims for every dollar collected in premiums, credit life insurers paid an average of 43.1 cents on the dollar in 1992.

Consumer-finance companies earn profits that make most businesses jealous. They routinely produce returns on assets that are three to four times what banks produce. It's no wonder major corporations such as NationsBank, Ford Motor Co. and defense contractor Textron have dived into this market. In Ohio, the big banks that have pushed their way into the state's consumer-finance trade include Norwest Corp., Banc One Corp., National City Corp. and Star Bank Corp.

Shark Bait
How some consumer-finance companies make a killing off people who badly need money.

Eric Rorer,
San Francisco Bay Guardian, **June 22, 1994**

For Abbe Patterson, October 17, 1989 was shaping up as a dream come true. She had box seats at the World Series on one of San Francisco's rare warm evenings. Her father, whom she had always wanted to take to a World Series game, was sitting by her side.

Patterson had worked hard to build a successful career in advertising. At 29, she was on her way, with a nice apartment in San Francisco's fashionable Marina District and a job with a fast-growing ad agency.

Then, just before game time, the Loma Prieta earthquake rumbled under Candlestick Park, suspending the World Series. And when Patterson arrived home several hours later, she discovered the quake had damaged much of her neighborhood and rendered her apartment uninhabitable. Within a year, Patterson was unemployed and living in a flea-infested residential hotel, stripped of almost all her possessions and cooking her meals in a toaster oven.

But Patterson doesn't blame the earthquake for her troubles. She says her biggest problem can be traced to a $2,000 loan she took out almost two years before the earthquake hit.

At the time, the loan didn't seem to be a big deal. Like many young people in the early stages of their careers, Patterson depended heavily on credit to maintain her lifestyle. And although she might not have qualified for a traditional bank loan, ITT was eager to advance her the cash.

When the earthquake upset her fragile financial equilibrium, Patterson now claims in a lawsuit, the ITT loan turned into a nightmare. For starters, she found out that she owed a lot more money than she'd expected—due, her suit claims, to some stiff hidden charges that weren't properly disclosed in the loan application. And while most of her creditors—Bank of America and her credit card companies—took the quake into account and gave her extra time to make payments, ITT collection agents called her and her friends and relatives night and day, at one point demanding that she send them her unemployment benefits.

More important, according to Patterson's lawsuit, she found that the ITT-affiliated renters' insurance that she thought was a part of the loan package wouldn't pay for most of her damaged property—and just when she needed the money the most, ITT withheld part of the insurance to pay off the outstanding loan.

Patterson isn't the only one complaining about ITT. In 1989, the company settled one of the largest consumer-fraud lawsuits in California history. Then-attorney general John Van de Kamp charged that company loan officers had tricked thousands of customers into buying unnecessary insurance service. As part of the settlement, ITT agreed to reimburse approximately $20 million to 40,000 customers.

In 1993, ITT decided to get out of the personal loan business altogether, so state officials now insist that they have the problem under control. Consumer advocates disagree. "We have always had suspicions about other companies," said Gail Hillebrand, an attorney for Consumers Union. "They've just never gotten busted. The sales tactics ITT has used are so lucrative that it's only common sense that other companies would want to use them."

In fact, a *Bay Guardian* investigation shows strong evidence that Hillebrand's suspicions are well founded.

I recently applied for loans at the local office of five major consumer-finance companies: American General Finance, Avco Financial Services, Beneficial of California, Household Finance, and ITT Financial Services (shortly before the company got out of the business). Although I didn't identify myself as a freelance journalist, all the other personal and financial information I provided to the loan officers was true and accurate.

My experience suggests that at least two of the companies, Avco and Beneficial, may be employing the same sorts of sales tactics Patterson says got her into trouble—and that forced ITT into its 1989 settlement with the state attorney general.

Gold mine

Although lending money to people who are marginal credit risks doesn't seem to be a promising business venture, the opportunities are good enough that the number of state licenses issued to practice such lending has more than doubled in recent years. There were 1,942 licensees as of 1985, and 5,008 as of September 1993, according to records on file with the state Department of Corporations, the agency in charge of regulating this kind of consumer lending.

According to a former ITT executive, Patterson was exactly the sort of person these companies were looking for. In 1986, Patterson badly needed some cash to fix her car, which she used for the hour-long commute to her job. An unsolicited notice she received in the mail told her that she qualified for a $2,000 loan—if she acted soon.

James Matthews, a former executive with both ITT and Avco, whose testimony was instrumental in Van de Kamp's settlement against the company, told the *Bay Guardian* that both of his former employers deliberately sought customers with low incomes or credit problems. Such customers, he said, are more desperate for money, and are willing to pay a higher price for it.

Matthews explained the situation in detail in a February 23, 1990, court deposition. "Solicitations were targeted for people who already have existing loans with finance companies or people who have limited credit," he stated. "As vice president/division director, I would review numerous loan files in the branch office under my supervision. Based upon the review of these files, including the customers' financial statements and credit reports, it was my understanding that most of [ITT's] customers were marginal credit risks."

Patterson had already taken a loan out from Bank of America and didn't think she would qualify for another conventional bank loan. "I didn't have bad credit," Patterson told the *Bay Guardian*. "But I didn't have a lot of credit."

ITT seemed like a legitimate, big-time operation,

Patterson said, so she didn't ask too many questions when she first went to the ITT office. "They were all very nice when I first went in," Patterson said.

When Patterson went to pick up the check the next day, however, she said ITT's offer got a bit more complicated. Holding the $2,000 check in conspicuous view, the loan agents explained she would need some insurance in order to take out the loan. "They told me it was renters' insurance," Patterson said. "I thought: 'Wow, they're doing me a favor. I'm covered. I don't need to go out and get renters' insurance.'"

But according to Patterson's October 1992 lawsuit, it wasn't exactly renters' insurance that ITT had sold her, but credit life insurance, credit disability insurance, and household contents insurance—for which ITT had charged her $484. Without having read the fine print of her contract, she said, she had no idea she had spent so much money. The ITT loan agents, Patterson's lawsuit alleges, never told her verbally about the extent of her insurance charges.

She made her monthly payments regularly, and according to the suit, after several months went by she got a call from ITT asking if she needed any more money. Because she had been able to keep up on her payments, and because she still wasn't suspicious of ITT, she decided to go ahead and accept their offer to refinance the loan. What she didn't realize was that included in the offer was another $659.81 in insurance premiums.

When the Loma Prieta quake destroyed her apartment, Patterson felt lucky; She remembered the ITT agents telling her she had renters' insurance. But her lawsuit alleges that when it came time to collect on that policy, she ran into a brick wall. It would take more than a year before she would get any money from ITT, the suit charges, and then she would get only $1,600 on a $5,000 claim for her household contents insurance.

That same year, the bottom fell out of the advertising industry because of a sharp downturn in the national economy, and Patterson was laid off only a few short months after the earthquake. She couldn't keep up payments on her ITT loan, or her Bank of America loan, or her credit cards. Because of the earthquake, everybody gave her leniency—except ITT.

"Everyone was very nice to me," Patterson said. "They were nice to everyone in the Marina, because they knew how bad things were there. Only ITT decided to make my life hell."

Four months after the earthquake, Patterson's suit charges, ITT officials began calling incessantly, demanding she pay back the money. "They called me 5, 10, sometimes even 15 times a day," she said.

In the summer of 1990, Patterson's suit claims, ITT officials told her they were about to pay off on her renters' insurance policy. Patterson, who had been living in a rented room near Golden Gate Park, decided to collect her security deposit, move to a cheap residential hotel, and find a new apartment the minute the insurance check arrived. But according to the lawsuit, ITT delayed payment until the end of 1990—and even then, the company refused to pay the full amount of the claim. Part of the insurance money was withheld to pay off some of Patterson's loan.

Things didn't turn around for Patterson until she sought help through the Legal Aid Society, a nonprofit group that gives free legal advice and referrals to people who can't afford to hire an attorney. Legal Aid sent her to Pat Sturdevant, a nationally renowned consumer-rights attorney based in San Francisco. It was only then that Patterson learned how much ITT had actually charged her for the insurance and other expenses.

Patterson became one of the lead plaintiffs in a class action lawsuit filed by Sturdevant that is still pending against ITT. Sturdevant says she hopes to take the 1989 lawsuit filed by the attorney general a step further.

While the settlement of the 1989 suit dealt almost entirely with fraudulent insurance sales, Sturdevant also wants to collect for harassment and false advertising—and to win reimbursement for a higher percentage of ITT's customers. Van de Kamp's suit only reached about 40,000 of the more than 250,000 Californians who had borrowed money from ITT.

Kristie Greve, a spokesperson for ITT's main office in Minneapolis, declined to comment on Patterson's allegations, saying the matter was under litigation.

Financial wonder

Companies like ITT Financial Service are legally classified by the State of California as "consumer financial lenders," or CFLs. CFLs differ from regular banks in that people don't invest or save money with them. That, consumer advocates say, means CFLs don't have to be federally insured—and thus escape most federal regulations.

The most significant result of this lack of regulation is that CFLs are allowed to underwrite and sell insurance in conjunction with loans. Although many of these companies charge interest rates as high as 30 percent, it's the insurance sales, not the high interest rates, that can make consumer lending a true gold mine.

"It's safe to say that for many of these companies, the actual loan is nothing more than a loss leader for the sale of ancillary insurance products," Kathleen Keest, a staff attorney with the National Consumer Law Center in Boston, told the *Bay Guardian*. "Customers who don't think they can get loans from banks are drawn in by the [CFL] loans and end up buying a whole bunch of insurance when they take out the loan."

The most common type of insurance sold to CFL customers in conjunction with loans is what is known as credit insurance. Although credit insurance has been around in one form or another for decades, it was in the early 1980s that it really came into vogue. The basic concept behind credit insurance is to pay off debts should a person lose the ability to pay off those debts through sickness, death, or involuntary unemployment, depending on what type of policy is purchased.

The product is sort of a financial wonder for finance companies, because including the insurance with a loan can often double the loan payments. Most small loans offered by CFLs have interest rates of around 25 percent, which isn't too much higher than what conventional banks charge for similar loans. With insurance charges, however, a loan from a CFL can require payments equivalent to 50 percent interest.

In addition, consumer advocates say, if customers ever make claims on their insurance policies, the insurance company doesn't pay the customer—it pays the finance company.

Because almost all the big finance companies sell their own insurance, or have subsidiaries that do, the companies usually end up paying themselves.

All of this is legal—with one important stipulation: Customers must be made fully aware that they aren't required to purchase the insurance in order to get a loan. The problem, Keest and other consumer advocates say, is that many customers are deliberately and systematically misled into buying the insurance either because they are led to believe it is required, or because the insurance charges are included in long, complex loan contracts that customers often sign without understanding them.

"I think the fact that the product [credit insurance] is purchased at the point of transaction [of a loan] is just inherently problematic," Nettie Hoge, a former attorney for Consumers Union who now works for the state Department of Insurance, told the *Bay Guardian*. "I personally think the product should be outlawed."

Still, state regulators say there's no big problem. "I think the majority of it [questionable business practices] has been stopped," Dale Lucas, chief examiner at the state Department of Corporations, said. "I think that suit sent a message throughout the state and the country.

"I don't think there are any bad players anymore," Lucas continued. "Even in Los Angeles now, with the earthquake, you don't see these companies trying to take advantage of people. They're trying to work with people."

The experience of this reporter tells a different story. In each of five loan applications submitted, I described my occupation—part-time word processor at an accounting firm—and asked for $1,500 for car repairs. Loan officers at Beneficial and Avco both used insurance-packing schemes similar to those that Abbe Patterson experienced with ITT.

At Avco, insurance charges were included in the loan contract, although I was never verbally notified of that fact. Careful reading of the contract showed $756 in charges that the agent never mentioned. When the charges were brought to the agent's attention, he said approval of the loan would have to be reconsidered if the charges were not included.

The Beneficial loan agent did not try to hide the insurance charges but offered no options that did not include them. At Beneficial, I was offered three different loan packages, all for $1,500, but each with a different array of insurance policies. All three options differed little in price, with payments ranging from $103 to $106 per month over a 24-month period, for a total payment of as much as $2,544—$1,044 in interest and other charges. That's closer to 57 percent than 25 percent. The extra cost, apparently, came from the loan insurance. When the agent was pressed as to whether the insurance charges were mandatory, she, like the Avco agent, said that without them approval of the loan would have to be reconsidered.

Calls to Avco headquarters in Irvine, California, were not returned.

Jean Luttringer, group vice president for Beneficial, told the *Bay Guardian*, "There is no mandatory requirement for insurance on any of the loans we make."

"We, as a company, have not had a problem with the sale of insurance," he said. "We are subjected to audits by the Department of Corporations on an annual basis and have never had any problems. It is part and parcel to the sale of these products that the salesperson make sure that the customer understand that these insurance products are optional."

Lucas, of the Department of Corporations, said he was surprised by my experience. "I haven't heard this about either of these companies before," he said. "It seems to be against their company policies."

Lucas said CFLs are subjected to random audits on an annual basis. However, he said, we couldn't see any copies of the audits—they're "confidential."

Lucas said his department does not conduct undercover loan applications because it lacks the resources. He also said he wouldn't disclose the specific sales rates for insurance products in conjunction with the loans, saying they were not matters of public record.

Consumer advocates were not at all surprised by our findings. "The odd thing about these issues is that nobody walks into a lawyer's office and says, 'I've been ripped off by insurance packing,'" attorney Pat Sturdevant said. "It usually requires a lawyer or somebody closely familiar with this field of business to figure that out."

ITT's tough collection practices drove Abbe Patterson to seek legal help. Other companies have adopted a different strategy—they go after debtors in small claims court.

In the first six months of 1993, Beneficial filed 154 lawsuits in San Francisco small claims court against customers, some of whom, records show, were as little as two months behind in their payments. That's more than one case every working day.

Luttringer said his company had little choice: "If they don't live up to their end of the contract, the alternative is small claims court," he said. "How far do we have to accept somebody not paying us?"

***

The Bottom Line

There was a pen in my hand, and across the table from me was a man with a shirt and tie on. The loan officer of the San Francisco office of Avco Financial Services wanted me to sign my name—and walk away with $1,500.

The Avco office was my first stop on a whirlwind loan-application tour of consumer finance lenders. I had embarked on the tour in order to find out firsthand how these companies do business.

As a part-time word processor making roughly $1,000 a month, I was a perfect candidate for these businesses, which target low-income customers. I asked each company for $1,500 and said I was going to use the money for new tires and a stereo for my car.

After much wrangling, the Avco executive finally agreed to show me a copy of the loan contract. It wasn't easy: First he wanted me to sign several documents, which he said were simply preliminary financial-disclosure papers that didn't obligate me to anything. But I had been warned by several attorneys from different consumer groups not to sign anything, period. So I insisted on seeing the actual contract before putting pen to paper.

The man from Avco already had a copy of my credit

report, my addresses and phone numbers for home and work, my parents' addresses and phone numbers, a copy of my driver's license, and a copy of my last paycheck. He also told me that, because the loan was going to be secured by my car, he would have to take and keep the title before I got the loan, even though the low blue-book value of the car is $7,000— more than four times the amount of the loan.

"Perhaps after you've paid off a thousand bucks or so you can come in and get it [the title] back," he said.

He showed me the contract and pointed to the numbers at the top of the document: A $1,500 loan at 24.5 percent interest with a monthly payment of $80 for three years, resulting in a total payoff of $2,880. Although I couldn't verify it at the time, those numbers don't make sense: A *Bay Guardian* computer analysis shows that at 24.5 percent interest, the monthly payments should be just over $59, with a total payoff of $2,124. Payments of $80 per month for 36 months add up to just under 49 percent interest on a loan of $1,500.

All told, there were $756 in charges for things that the loan officer never said anything about, and although I didn't know it as I sat across from him, I knew to look for charges that seemed unusual. Scanning the contract, I saw a box marked "credit insurance," with a charge of $281.69, and another box marked "NEWPORT" with a charge of $220.

I pointed to the credit insurance charge and asked what it was all about.

"Oh, that protects you," he explained. "In case anything happens to you, if you get injured or sick, or if you get into an accident playing sports—you look pretty athletic—then this protects you."

I then asked about the box marked "NEWPORT."

"Oh, this is for the car. In case anything happens to the car; if you get into an accident, or if it's stolen or something, then this protects you."

He asked me if I was uncomfortable with the contract and said that if I thought the interest rate, 24.5 percent, was too high, he could talk to his manager and possibly get it lowered. I told him I wanted to think about the deal and asked him if it would be OK if I took a copy of the contract home with me to look over.

"That's against company policy," he said.

"Why?" I asked.

"That's just the policy the company has," he said.

I asked if I could just copy down the interest rate, the monthly payment, and the number of payments from the contract. Again he said that would be against company policy. So I memorized them and wrote them down as soon as I stepped out of the office.

The loan officer called me the next day to see if I still wanted the loan. I started asking him more questions about the insurance. I asked him if there was any way I could get the loan without the insurance.

"Well, that [insurance] is a protection, and that is how the loan was approved," he said.

Knowing that it was illegal to require that I buy the insurance, I pressed him on it. Again the loan officer said that the loan had been approved with the insurance charges included, but that he would check with his "manager" to find out if I could get a loan without them. He put me on hold and was gone for perhaps a minute. When he came back on, he said I could have the loan without the credit insurance but that I would still have to buy the auto insurance because I was using the car as collateral.

"I have to have that [auto insurance] even if the car is already insured?" I asked.

"Do you have full coverage?" he asked in return, having never inquired about this before.

"No, I have comprehensive liability," I answered.

"See, that's why," he said.

Later, when I checked the legality of this claim with the California Department of Insurance, I was told that because the car was being used as collateral, Avco could legally require that I have collision insurance in addition to what I already have, but that I could just upgrade my already existing policy instead of buying a new one from Avco.

I told the loan officer that I couldn't afford the extra charges on the loan and that I was going to pass on his offer. He called three more times, although each time I told him I wasn't interested.

I had a somewhat similar experience when I visited a local Beneficial office, where I was offered a $1,500 loan—at 25.3 percent—with monthly payments of $106 over two years. The Beneficial loan agent was up front about the insurance charges, but she never mentioned that they were optional. A computer analysis shows that the actual interest rate for the payments would be closer to 57 percent.

During a later visit to a Household Finance office, an account representative inadvertently gave me an insight into the whole situation. When I applied for a loan with Household, I asked if I could take the loan contract home with me before signing it. "Have you read the agreements on your two credit cards?" the representative asked. "Because this is basically the same as those."

In a fit of defensive instinct, I claimed I had read those agreements. The truth, however, is that I never have. To this day, I still don't even know where they are.

Editor's Epilogue

ITT Corp. settled the private class action over its credit-insurance practices in California by paying about $4 million in refunds. ITT has sold off almost all of its lending units.

"Signing Their Lives Away"

Ford Profits Big from Vulnerable Consumers

Michael Hudson, 1996

PHILIP WHITE had been working at Associates Financial Services a few months before his dad looked at him and said, "Son, I don't know how you can look yourself in the mirror, doing what you're doing." White told his dad: "Look, it's a job and I'm just doing what I'm told.... I'm just a spoke in the wheel."

White hadn't thought his first real job would be like that. The summer of 1991, he was 21. He'd had a bit of college, then served as a Navy medic on the ground with the Marines in the Gulf War. He was ready for a career. He got a job as a loan officer in Alabama with Associates, a huge national company that makes personal loans and mortgages to people with modest incomes or bad credit histories. It was owned by Ford Motor Co., and had an impressive—and profitable—history. White thought it was a great job.

He found out different. He entered a world, he says, where cunning and deception were standard tools of the trade, where customers were routinely snowed by confusing paperwork and sleight-of-hand salesmanship.

It started with persistent pressure to close the loan. Many customers didn't—or couldn't—read their loan documents. White says they frequently never saw forms disclosing broker's fees, and loan officers often added in hundreds, even thousands of dollars in charges for credit insurance—without asking them if they needed it. White says higher-ups told him, "If you don't have to tell 'em and they don't ask, don't tell 'em. Just get 'em to initial it. They're big people. They can read—most of them anyway." White, who eventually rose to assistant branch manager, claims customers were also misled about upfront points and other finance charges. The attitude was: "If you had to lie about the points that we charged, lie to 'em. They're stupid anyway."

If customers fell behind on their payments, he says, you

were expected to refinance their loans to jack up their interest rates and debt. When they were panicky and in the hole, he says, you could get them to sign just about anything. They had a name for this around the office: "Nut-squeezing."

***

MENTION FORD MOTOR CO. and most people think: Mustang, Escort, Taurus, Ranger, Aerostar. But building cars, trucks and vans isn't what's put Ford near the top of the Fortune 500 list in recent years. What pushed it so high? Banking and consumer lending.

The business press has called Ford's financial services empire the engine that makes the company go—even its savior during rocky times in the auto business. In 1993, three-fifths of Ford's earnings came from its financial services subsidiaries. The biggest earner among it credit units is Ford Motor Credit Corp., but a large chunk of its profits come from a lesser-known subsidiary, Associates Corp. of North America. In 1994, the Dallas-based company made $18.5 billion in mortgages and consumer loans and earned just under $1 billion in pre-tax profits. "There are 25 to 30 million households in the U.S. that do not have banking relationships—that's where Associates does its work," banking analyst Jim Hanbury told *Automotive News*. "Associates offers good service to the blue-collar, urban and small-town customer base ... the banks refuse to work with."

Not everyone agrees about the benefits that flow from being in Ford Motor Co.'s debt. In fact, Ford has become the target of lawsuits across the nation charging it with cheating disadvantaged borrowers. The allegations include trickery, fraud, and forgery. In Arizona, for example, Associates paid almost $3.4 million to settle charges it had manipulated customers into buying high-priced insurance with their loans. And Ford Motor Credit has agreed to pay more than $120 million to settle charges that it had "force-placed" overpriced accident insurance onto the loans of borrowers who had let their original insurance lapse. The lawsuits against the auto company's various lending arms have involved at least three-quarters of a million customers across the United States. "They're raping and pillaging," says Terry Drent, a community activist in Ann Arbor, Michigan, who has been investigating Associates' links to home-repair companies in Michigan and Ohio. "It's amazing to me that this top Fortune 500 company is basically based on greed and sleazy tactics."

So far the charges against the company haven't received national attention. Ford concedes no chicanery in any of the cases, including the ones it has settled. In the Ford Motor Credit case, for example, a spokesman said the company was worried about "the risk of a runaway jury verdict." Industry observers contend Ford's financial empire is the victim of greedy trial attorneys looking for a payday—and of overzealous juries. "In the big picture, we serve millions of customers and serve them well," one Associates spokesman said. "We live in a litigious society and there are going to be lawsuits, no matter what your business." Another Associates spokesman, Fred Stern, dismissed Philip White's allegations as groundless, and said White failed to show up when the company's lawyers tried to get a sworn statement from him.

Despite the denials, it's hard to scratch the surface of Ford's credit empire without finding allegations of abuse. Take First Family Financial Services, a growing consumer lender in the Southeastern United States that was purchased by Associates Corp. in 1992. First Family paid an estimated $3.5 million in 1995 to settle a lawsuit that accused it of fleecing about 2,500 Alabama borrowers. The class action claimed the company paid secret kickbacks to brokers to encourage them to steer homeowners into higher-cost loans. In early 1996 it settled another Alabama lawsuit accusing it of overcharging about three dozen borrowers on credit insurance.

In Jacksonville, Florida, a lawsuit alleged First Family had taken advantage of an elderly black woman who was having trouble handling her finances. It started when a home-repair company persuaded Mattie Foster, 72, to sign a contract for a new roof and new carpet. According to the lawsuit, the roof work was poor—rain soon was leaking in—and she never got the carpet. What she did get was a loan with First Family.

The repair company arranged for a loan for her through the lender. She was charged a $1,700 broker's fee to get $4,380 to cover the home repairs. The lender also paid off her original mortgage, bringing her total debt to First Family to $18,000.

From 1990 to 1994, First Family persuaded her to refinance four times—each time giving her a bit of new money but charging her much more in closing costs. On one loan, she received $25.66 in new money but paid more than *20 times* that in closing costs—$524.47. She ended up with a $22,000 mortgage on her home at 18 percent interest. Her $385-a-month mortgage payments were more than half her Social Security income.

Mattie Foster is now in the early stages of Alzheimer's. The only reason First Family didn't get her to sign a sixth loan was her daughter stepped in and stopped it. A local Legal Aid clinic sued, charging First Family with fraud. The lender denied any double-dealing, but agreed to pay Mattie Foster a settlement that included wiping out her mortgage so she could own her home free and clear.

****

The folks at Associates say critics simply don't understand the nature of the business. "There may be a misunderstanding," says Bob Williams, manager of the company's Roanoke, Virginia, branch. "They feel like we're gouging the customer. [But] a lot of people need our services. All we're trying to provide is a service to people who might not be able to get credit elsewhere—and let them have the opportunity that an upper class person might have." Williams says many of his customers are likely to be rejected by banks or credit-card companies. "We may take an extra chance," he says. "They're willing to pay a little bit higher rate for us to take a chance."

Williams says the kinds of abuses White describes simply don't happen at Associates. He says the company never sells credit insurance to customers who don't want it. And he says it's careful to check out the background of the home-repair contractors and other companies that feed it loan business.

Lawsuits filed across the nation, however, paint a less appealing picture of the company—from the Pacific Northwest, to the American Southwest, to Philadelphia, to both coasts of Florida. A few examples:

• In 1993 Associates agreed to pay $3 million to about 8,000 low- and moderate-income borrowers in Arizona to settle a lawsuit accusing it of illegally packing credit insurance into their contracts. It paid another $375,000 to Arizona's attorney general.

• In 1990, the company agreed to pay up to $230,000 to settle a class-action lawsuit in South Carolina claiming Associates had used complex loan provisions to overcharge borrowers on interest.

• In 1991, Associates Credit Card Services agreed to pay $48,000 to settle allegations by the Texas attorney general's office that its collectors had harassed 56 debtors by calling them repeatedly, cursing at them, and calling their co-workers and bosses. "We felt that there were some instances that could have been handled in a different manner," a company spokesman said.

• In 1992, Associates paid cash to settle a lawsuit in Washington state charging it with forging loan papers. It also settled a 1988 Seattle-area lawsuit charging Associates had bamboozled a couple into refinancing a lower-interest loan with another lender for an 18.25 percent mortgage with Associates.

• In 1994, an Alabama jury slammed Associates with a $34.5 million verdict for trying to foreclose on a customer, Rosa Davis, who claimed her name had been forged on loan papers. Two other customers testified they believed their loan papers had also been forged. Associates said no one's papers were forged.

The judge ordered a retrial in the Davis case, saying he had made a mistake by letting her attorneys describe Associates as a company without conscience. Before the new trial, Associates settled for an undisclosed sum.

The settlement came after Philip White's name appeared on a witness list for Davis. White didn't know Davis, but he told her attorneys that he knew of document forgeries in the two Associates offices he worked at in Alabama. He says these included "truth-in-lending" disclosure forms, which tell borrowers exactly how much they're borrowing and what their interest rate is. He claims personally to know of at least 20 to 25 instances in which customers' signatures were forged. Associates' Stern says that after hearing about White's forgery allegations, the company sent its auditors into the two branches where White had worked and "they found no basis for his allegations—none whatsoever."

A former Associates branch manager east of the Mississippi says it's common practice for employees to fill in customers' signatures on documents, but only if the customer OK's it over the phone or if it's an innocuous document that won't hurt them. The ex-manager, who spoke on the condition his name not be revealed, believes the company "crosses the 't's' and dots the 'i's' of the law." But what's more important, he says, is this: Does it treat its customers fairly? Not usually, he says. "The sales methods are so deceiving." He says that, with all the numbers and documents involved, it's easy for a loan officer to throw out some figures and say, "I can save you $25,000, isn't that great?" The loan officer nods his head up and down and makes eye contact. The bewildered customers nod their heads yes too. "They'll be signing their lives away," this manager says. It's not until too late that they suddenly realize, "I have an $800-a-month house payment."

He says the company sold credit-insurance—which is supposed to cover the loan if borrowers die, get sick or lose their jobs—under "the doctrine of assumed consent." Loan officers wrote it into contracts without asking, he claims, and only removed it if the customer noticed and vigorously objected. The insurance is lucrative for Associates, often doubly so when it's purchased from companies that are controlled by—you guessed it—Associates.

"That insurance is just pure profit," says Philip White. "It's something they want you to sell on every loan. If you don't, you definitely have some problems, some pressures put on you. That was one of the main things: At all costs do it. What are you gonna do? You want to keep your job."

Both White and the former branch manager say employees were under enormous pressure to grow—to make more loans, sell more insurance, bolster profits. "Some of the people there are very nice," White says. "They're put under such immense pressure to produce profits that everybody knows what's going on. .... The people are good but they do things they don't want to."

"The pressure came from the top," the ex-manager said. "You have to take some short cuts.... I did some things that were risky—loans that I didn't want to do—just to grow."

Associates certainly has grown—at an astounding pace of nearly 20 percent a year. From the time Ford bought Associates in 1989 to the end of 1994, it more than doubled in size—to 13,734 employees and $32.2 billion in assets. One way the company has grown is by working with home-repair contractors, appliance stores, electronic dealers and other independent businesses to bring in new customers. "That feeds us business," says Williams, the Roanoke branch manager. These businesses sign people to credit contracts and then sell the contracts to Associates. Then Associates tries to persuade their new customers to borrow more money. In some cases, small loan contracts get ratcheted into much larger loans—and a mortgage on the customer's home. That's what happened to Ruth Williams.

Williams, 65, was earning about $6,000 a year as a cafeteria worker in Jupiter, Florida. A widow, she owned her house free and clear but had little else to her name. She got into hock with Associates after buying a washing machine on credit. The lender mailed her a solicitation saying she could borrow more money: "Combine your debts, get extra cash at no extra cost!"

She bit. The company gave her $9,085 in cash, paid off $9,909 in other debts and charged her $3,123 for credit insurance and $1,849 as an up-front loan fee. Then it refinanced her loan twice more—each time assessing a "pre-payment penalty" on the previous loan and then adding thousands more in insurance and fees. In the end, she found herself with a 17-percent mortgage on her home totaling more than $37,000. She couldn't make the monthly payments and Associates tried to foreclose. She countersued. Her attorney said in the lawsuit that the promise of more money at "no extra cost" had been a lie, and that Associates knew Williams didn't understand the papers she signed. Associates is fighting the allegations.

Associates' sister company, Ford Motor Credit, serves a wider range of consumers. But the better-known company's legal entanglements have also stemmed largely from the way it has treated less-advantaged borrowers like Ruth Williams.

During the 1980s, Ford Motor Credit and dozens of other lenders nationwide began pushing an obscure product called "force-placed auto insurance." It worked like this: When you let your auto insurance lapse, the lender that holds a lien on your title has the right to buy insurance to cover itself in case of accident. The lender can add the price of the insurance onto the loan. Ford and many other auto lenders were accused of buying much more insurance than was necessary and tacking on illegal charges to jack up the price—and thus the interest they could earn on padded loan amounts. Ford was also accused of taking kickbacks from insurers as an incentive for inflating the insurance. Borrowers' attorneys say the victims were typically people with modest educations and incomes—consumers who were likely to be unable to afford to keep their insurance current and more likely not to understand the complex documents notifying them of the "force-placed" insurance.

***

SO FAR THE LEGAL problems at Ford's credit units haven't affected the bottom line. In 1994 Associates Corp.'s profits grew 17 percent as it posted record earnings for the 20th year in a row. "Associates' policy is that litigation doesn't matter," the former branch manager claims. "They'd rather not have it." But "if they get caught with their hand in the cookie jar, they can settle their way out of it."

Associates Corp. now controls more than 1,700 finance offices in the U.S., Mexico, Japan and the United Kingdom. The company says it "intends to remain on the cutting edge and continue reaching out to new markets." It now serves many U.S. communities where Chinese, Thai, Laotian, Spanish and even Portuguese are the primary languages, and tries to have as many bilingual employees as possible.

In 1993 a competitor, ITT Financial Services, closed hundreds of its offices amid heavy financial losses and a slew of loan-fraud lawsuits that cost it $80 million—cases that alleged credit-insurance packing and other complaints similar to those leveled at Associates. With ITT out of the picture, Associates moved to fill the void. It hired 670 ex-ITT employees and opened 170 new offices, many of them in places abandoned by

ITT. Tom Slone, president of Associates' U.S. operations, said the new locations would give it a chance to build "from the ground up" in small towns and other places not yet served by Associates. "It's a courageous undertaking for our people," he said.

Philip White is a bit more sanguine when it comes to Associates. He says he got tired of having to threaten and cajole debtors. When people were behind on their payments, he says, his bosses "wanted me to be an asshole." He recalls going out with co-workers on a collection call a few days before Christmas. They told the family, "Get your Christmas tree, get your presents, because we'll take you to a hotel. Because this is our house now." In desperation the customer borrowed money from relatives to pay Associates.

White says it was cases like that that made him want to come forward and tell his story. Company spokesman Stern says, "the circumstances of him leaving the company may be the reason for him saying these things. I can't say anything about that—and wouldn't in fairness to a former employee." White says he was rebuked for not being tough enough, and he resigned in early 1993 when it looked like Associates was going to fire him anyway.

It was a relief to leave, he says. He believes the practices that got Associates sued in Alabama are common, because the pressure to produce forces employees to violate the law—and customers' trust. "This is not a random act. This is an act that happens everywhere in Alabama, that happens everywhere in the U.S. It's not something like 'We made a mistake and slipped.' "

After leaving Associates, he worked for a few months for another national lender—United Companies Financial Corp.— that has also been accused of bleeding low-income borrowers. It's not just Associates that takes advantage, White says. "It's everybody. It's the industry as a whole that needs to be changed."

Part III
The Shadow Banks:
Pawnshops and Check Cashers

Pawnshops and check-cashing outlets cater to the "nonbank" market—perhaps 50 million to 60 million consumers who aren't regular bank customers. Many avoid banks out of distrust, but many have been driven away from banks by rising fees and monthly balance requirements. In recent years, bank fees have risen at twice the rate of inflation, according to U.S. Public Interest Research Group. Bounced check fees—which are as high as $30 in some places—now average 7 1/2 times what it costs banks to process a bad check. Many people say the fear of bounced checks keeps them from opening accounts.

If you're poor, getting a bank account can be a struggle. Pacquin Davis found that out a few years ago. She had been taking her welfare check to a market around the corner, paying $3 to cash a $390 check. When she needed extra money, she went to a pawnshop downtown, paying $15 interest each month on a $75 loan—an annual rate of 240 percent.

She decided to break away from these "fringe banks." Davis went to two Atlanta banks to open an account, but they turned her away because a furniture store had left a bad mark on her credit. One refused even to allow her to open a savings account. She kept trying—with the support of a sympathetic Legal Aid attorney—and finally went to a third bank that opened an account. She was happy to have a real bank, but the earlier rejections were painful—the kind of first-time experience that might turn a less-determined consumer off on banks for good. "They just put that fear in your heart," she said. "It kinda scares you to walk in that door."

'Fringe Banks' Profit from Customers Without Banks

Mary Kane,
Newhouse News Service, April 1992

It's just after quitting time when Bob Platt pulls into the parking lot of the Check Exchange, a storefront along a busy Atlanta highway. Still in his work clothes—dirt-stained blue jeans and a T-shirt—Platt strides inside and cashes his $32 paycheck.

He shells out $1 for the privilege. As he climbs back into his pickup, Platt says he hates paying the fee but there's nothing he can do. He's a day laborer, and without steady work he can't open a bank account.

"They just don't want you," he says, shaking his head.

All afternoon, the scene is repeated. Jose Mendez finishes his shift as a cashier at Taco Bell and pays $3 to cash his $60 weekly paycheck. Ron Scholfield, a salesman, pays $20 to cash a $200 money order.

For more and more Americans, this is banking in the '90s. Living from paycheck to paycheck, they find it difficult to meet the credit requirements and minimum balances necessary for a checking account.

At least 14 percent of all American families no longer have a bank account, up from 9 percent in 1977, according to the Federal Reserve.

To fill the void, the check-cashing stores have doubled in number in just five years. Also booming are pawnshops, where people who can't get credit cards or bank loans pay up to 240 percent interest for small loans.

"It's scandalous," said Troy Smith, an attorney with the Homeowners Outreach Center in Los Angeles, which represents the financial interests of low-income people. "The people who can least afford to pay are being charged excessive and exorbitant amounts. These are people who need every penny they can get. Ten dollars is a lot to them."

Check-cashers and pawnshop owners say they're not to

blame; they have no choice but to charge more for checks and loans that banks might not touch.

"If there wasn't a need we wouldn't be here," said Mike Shelton, who owns a chain of five check-cashing stores in suburban Atlanta. "These people aren't served by banks. Where are they going to go?"

As their popularity has increased, check-cashing stores have spread from the inner city to working-class and suburban neighborhoods. And they've expanded from mom-and-pop operations into major businesses.

Cash America International, a chain with almost 200 stores, is among five pawnshop chains traded publicly; its stock has tripled since the mid '80s. Major investors include a British insurance company and First Interstate Bank Corp. of Los Angeles, which owns 7 percent. Western Union is launching a nationwide chain of 500 to 1,000 check-cashing stores.

"Fringe Banks" is how some economists describe these businesses. They don't make real estate loans, don't provide a place for people to keep their savings, and don't establish the kind of community stability that draws other business.

Poverty rights advocates such as Acorn, the Association of Community Organizations for Reform Now, are concerned about the larger effects of this growth.

"It's creating two financial systems for two Americas," contends Chris Lewis, an organizer with Acorn's national office in Washington. "One for the rich and one for the poor."

Popping up on the suburban landscape among the fast-food restaurants, outlet malls and car dealerships are places such as Pawns R Us, EZ Pawn, Check Exchange, and EZ Check Cashing. Billboards and neon signs blare a simple sales pitch: Bad Credit No Problem. No ID Necessary.

Check-cashers took in about $790 million in fees during 1990, according to industry estimates, while pawnshops made about $37 million in loans. Cash America's profits have risen by 2 percent each year since it went public in 1987.

Howard Mandelbaum, spokesman for the National Check Cashers Association, said people are turning away from banks because "the hours are lousy, the convenience isn't there, and you get your money right away at a check-casher."

"Banks have walked away from the real small customer," added Gene Estep, vice president of Cash America. "If you don't want to borrow at least $10,000 they don't want you."

Deregulation in 1980 opened the door for banks to charge more for accounts with small balances and for bounced checks.

During the 1970s and '80s, many banks also closed branches in poor neighborhoods. According to a study by Swarthmore College economist John P. Caskey, neighborhoods with large concentrations of blacks or poor people are half as likely as other neighborhoods to have a local bank branch.

South Central Los Angeles, a low-income minority community of 400,000 people, is typical of the trend: it has only 19 bank branches but 133 check-cashing stores.

All told, the percentage of poor families without checking or savings accounts grew from 28 percent to 45 percent between 1977 and 1989, according to the Federal Reserve.

Michael Griffin, a bank executive and representative of the American Banker's Association, called it "bank-bashing" to accuse banks of pricing out the poor. He points to an ABA study that found the percentage of banks offering low-cost accounts increased from 44 percent in 1987 to 59 percent by 1990.

Griffin said a certain percentage of the population simply can't be served by banks, and will continue to provide a market for check-cashers and pawnbrokers.

"Will we ever totally eliminate the need for those people? I just don't see it."

Pawnbrokers and check-cashers say the reasons people use them vary, but most customers have some kind of chink in their financial armor. Bad credit. No ID. No steady job.

At the drive-through window of EZ Check Cashing in the Atlanta suburb of Norcross, a woman pulls up, explains she can't read or write and asks for help cashing her check.

Bill Lavelle, a New Jersey salesman who just moved to Atlanta, says he cashes his check here because he's in the midst of a divorce and doesn't want to let his wife's lawyer know where his money is.

Sara Jenkins, 30, an electrical engineer who earns more

than $40,000 per year, says her bank mishandled a direct deposit, her checks bounced, and she had to cover the costs. She hasn't had a checking account in three years.

Whatever the reason they use them, customers of check-cashing stores pay more for their services. A family of four with an income of $24,000 per year would pay $396 annually if it cashed its paychecks at a check-cashing store and bought six money orders per month, according to Caskey's calculations.

That same family could have a free checking account at a bank—if they could maintain a minimum balance requirement that averaged $481 in 1990, according to the Consumer Federation of America.

But they would be subject to monthly maintenance fees of $5 to $10 whenever the balance fell below the required minimum. And fees for bounced checks average $15 and can run as high as $25.

Check-cashing stores became established in the 1940s, first appearing in Chicago and New York. It wasn't until the last decade that they began to spread to other cities. Pawnshops have been around since the turn of the century, but they also had been in decline until the mid '80s.

Since 1986, nationwide listings for pawnshops have jumped by 60 percent, totaling 7,760 by 1991, according to American Business Information. Check-cashing stores have more than doubled from 2,151 in 1987 to 4,289 at the end of 1990.

Only seven states limit fees charged by check-cashing stores, and even these regulations aren't always honored. Officials in New Jersey discovered in a survey that 49 percent of a sample of customers at check-cashing stores were charged more than the legal maximum.

Most states, however, regulate pawnshops, with interest rates ranging from 3 percent to 20 percent per month—or 240 percent per year.

The economics of a typical pawnshop work this way: Don't pay and you lose what you pawned. Or pay the interest and reclaim your possession. Either way, nothing goes on your credit record.

At EZ Pawn in suburban Norcross, classical music plays in the background. The inside is carpeted and lined with glass cases where pawned merchandise is neatly displayed. Ernest Royal, the owner, points to a computer a young woman pawned the night before.

"She said she'd bought it to do her doctoral dissertation," he said.

When he opened his shop three years ago, Royal handled 2,400 pawns a year. In the past year, he's handled 4,500.

Banks don't make any small consumer loans anymore, he said, and people who have spotty credit histories can't get them anyway. Throw in the recession and you can see why pawnshops are taking off.

"I'd say 10 to 15 percent of my customers are people who've been laid off. Lots of them are used to making large amounts of money. They've got lots of valuable possessions. What they don't have anymore is a paycheck."

Joanne Saracina, 26, and her daughter, Jessica, 4, visited Royal's shop not long ago. Saracina and her husband are self-employed painting contractors. Because of recent rains, business has been slow. They pawned an air compressor for $100 to pay the utility bill.

"It costs us $27 to do it, but it's either that or not pay a major bill," she said.

In some cities, neighborhood grocery stores, liquor stores and other businesses have a long tradition of cashing checks for free for regular customers. But the boom in the check-cashing industry has prompted many of these businesses to begin charging.

For some stores, check-cashing has grown into a lucrative sideline. One of the biggest check-cashers in the working-class Atlanta suburb of Doraville is the Tower Package store.

The rate schedule—posted above the checkout line for beer and liquor—notes that it costs $1.65 to cash a check for up to $200, but offers 50 cents off if you buy $5 worth of alcohol.

This also disturbs critics of the check-cashing business, who contend it encourages wasteful spending among people who have little extra income to begin with.

"The thing that really gets me is, when you walk into the

store, the first thing you see is a lottery ticket for sale and cigarettes all over the place," said Louis Krouse, chairman of the National Partnership for Social Enterprise, a nonprofit corporation that encourages businesses to address social problems.

"How much social engineering are we supposed to do?" asked Mandelbaum of the National Check Cashers Association. "People are going to buy their lottery ticket anyway. Is it more or less moral if they buy from a check-cashing store?"

Reformers have no shortage of ideas for improving financial services for the poor.

Many have suggested setting reasonable limits on fees charged by fringe bankers. Beyond that, groups such as Acorn have been lobbying for legislation that would require banks to provide basic low-cost accounts.

Such legislation has been introduced in Congress regularly for the past 10 years, but has met with no success.

"The banks have been the problem," said Nancy Coffey, spokeswoman for Sen. Howard Metzenbaum, D-Ohio, who sponsored the most recent legislation. "They're not interested in having poor people as customers."

Some bankers have taken steps on their own to serve more low-income customers. In Massachusetts, some banks have agreed to cash government checks for non-customers; in Cincinnati, banks are taking on low-income customers who lack conventional credit histories by reviewing their rent and other payments as alternative credit references.

But Caskey and other experts foresee no slowdown in the growth of fringe banks. Indeed, both pawnshops and check-cashing stores have begun offering additional financial service. Many pawnshops also cash checks, sell money orders and handle income tax returns. Check-cashing stores frequently offer money transfers from Western Union and American Express. (The usual fee: $15 to send the first $100.)

Customers believe they have no alternative.

"Sometimes I feel like it's a little too much," said Geneva Harris, a nurse who patronizes EZ Check Cashing. "But it's the price you have to pay."

Prince of Pawns

With a keen appreciation for the high-return, low-risk investment, Jack Daugherty is making hock shops a hot corporate property

Bill Minutaglio,
The Dallas Morning News, **December 4, 1988**

This place, this final repository for a million surrendered dreams, has a real nice parking lot—with a little sign advising that keeping your car there can set you back $10.

It is a few steps to a dimly lit elevator adorned with a startling notice: In a few hours there will be a lunch for "gentlemen only" in the Hunt Grille-Pub. And on the 10th floor are the soft hums of efficiency, parquet floors and walls tinted the color of cash.

There, at the soothing conclusion of a deep-carpeted hallway and nestled amid Oriental vases and oil paintings, sits the master gardener for a tawdry, inescapable piece of American cultural kudzu. Here, in the mustily elegant Fort Worth Club building, is the most powerful pawnbroker in the world.

But there is no jeweler's glass. No weathered, mismatched gathering of golf clubs. No wire-cage windows, rickety steel shelves crammed with blackened hot plates, no eight-track stereo parts. Not one cracked pocket watch. Italian accordion. Plastic popcorn popper.

Instead there is a huge, daunting, scary man who sounds like John Wayne speaking from the bottom of a deep well: "Five years ago, if you said pawnshops at one of the local country clubs, they would whisper. They wouldn't even talk to you. If I had gone to an investment banking firm like Dean Witter or Merrill Lynch they would have thrown me out."

Jack Daugherty, with an oval-shaped head topped with a divot of hair resting on a sandtrap of scalp, lets his aggressive chant settle. So far, he has amassed 100 pawnshops. He wants more.

His company, Cash America Investments, Inc., is the first and only one of its kind traded on the stock market. When stockbrokers punch up information on their Quotrons about his company, it is listed on their American Stock Exchange rosters as "PWN." (It's listed as CshAm in newspaper listings.)

"They" have learned that in five years Daugherty's company went from $16,000 in equity to $80 million; $35,000 in revenues to $60 million.

Finally, for good parts of 1988, Daugherty, 42, toyed with the thought of acquiring ColorTyme Corp., the largest rent-to-own conglomeration in the nation, with 500 franchises in 36 states. Though he eventually dropped the plan because he didn't like ColorTyme's current structure, the move gusted Daugherty's name through investment houses and business publications as one of the very few, new, intimidating cleanup hitters from Texas.

It is also directing attention to what may be Daugherty's attempt to reinvent an infamous wheel. By monopolizing a long-standing, disparaged, underground economy of pawns and rentals. By making money in a huge, maligned financial system that runs without the grease that banks usually ooze.

"We know that there are 50 to 70 million Americans who could use our services," resonates the pawnbroker. Daugherty stares hard to see if these numbers are getting through. "The chance for this to be a growing business is unbelievable. It is awesome."

In 1987, when Daugherty took his company public, his firm surged forward as the third-best-performing initial public offering in the nation, No. 1 in Texas. Offered at $10, it rolled to $18 a share and settled back into the $12 range this autumn.

People liked where Daugherty was coming from: Under this state's generous—some argue usurious—laws, pawnshops can command as much as a staggering 240 percent interest a year from people hocking their possessions.

Today, Daugherty's office hands out a photocopy that shows two newspaper stories from the same business page. One is headlined "BankAmerica Reports Loss of $1.1 Billion." The other is headlines "Cash America Had Earnings Gain of

300 Percent in Second Quarter." If profits continue to roll, its possible income could be well over $5 million at the end of the year, almost double 1987's profits.

Overseas, where pawnshops don't sag under as scurrilous a reputation, investors are falling all over themselves to get to Daugherty and snap up shares. More than 50 percent of the stock is owned by foreign, principally European, speculators.

All this for places that most people blow by on the highway. Places that often seem, at least in Texas, set back across the tracks and tied to the era of the last picture show. Rambling, taken-for-granted mausoleums filled with varsity football prizes, a stuffed javelin over the door and barbed-wire letters spelling out promises of cash-in-a-flash.

Pawns, if you don't have to use them, are always there on the edge. Always existing on the dark peripheries of respectability. Inescapable outskirt enterprises, exiled near no-tell motels and burglar-barred liquor stores.

But pawns, if you do have to use them, are the ultimate poor man's bank. Hard-core alternative commercial reality for millions of gimmie cappers—millions of the calloused who remain exiled outside the shiny revolving door. The people who don't deal with banks because the banks won't let them.

Pawns can also be something else: Places that summon uncomfortable thoughts of desperate families confronting and finally submitting to ice-hearted usury. Thoughts of people offering the pawn man the few concrete things that define their lives—Rod Steiger loaning $2 for the shattered man's priceless oratory trophy in *The Pawnbroker*. And finally, thoughts of finding your grandmother's stolen glass eyes staring at you from a cheap, blinking window display.

There are 7,000 of them in the United States. Seven thousand money-lending institutions that draw their lifeblood from the unforgiving purity of unemployment, secondhand things and hard coinage.

And it is not by accident that Jack Daugherty, chairman and chief executive officer, elected to call his operation Cash America Investments, Inc. Each of his 100 pawnshops has an average, on any given day, of $120,000 in outstanding loans—

and Daugherty adamantly insists that you not call them loans and interest, but "service charges" for holding property.

"We don't foreclose on him. We don't ruin his credit rating like a bank can do. And where else can the little guy get cash on short notice?" demands Daugherty, leaning forward in his leather chair, his voice full of chinny defiance. "Do you know what you do with a pawn in chess? You put it at risk. In pawnshops, all people put at risk are the things they bring in. That's all."

But in Texas, where the state's biggest banks handed out as many bad loans as greed would allow, Daugherty himself has put very little at risk. In pawnshops, as people at Cash America have proudly pointed out, there is no such thing as a bad loan. If you default, the pawnshop simply sells your precious heirloom. And it is sold as fast as possible and for more than you were loaned.

The fact that Daugherty has cheerfully acknowledged the chilly beauty of owning a big chunk of that system is not what is surprising. It is the fact that someone didn't successfully do it sooner. Someone else, say, who is also from Texas—the classic breeding ground for a diverse legion of we-make-the-rules capitalists from Billie Sol Estes to T. Boone Pickens, from the Hunt Brothers to H. Ross Perot.

But Daugherty it is. And he is restructuring and corralling a non-bank system that has 50 million potential customers, one that could suck strength from mass fears and hatred of banks, one that could cause more than a few to rethink the wonderful world of credit, loans and savings.

Daugherty gets positively spiritual when he looks at the possible big picture. This is the second time we have met and talked. This is the first time he has drifted away from peroration and into the higher harmony of the hocked.

"Do you mind if I say something?" Daugherty drawls while waving his hand. For the last hour, he has been sharply steering the conversation wherever he wants. Permission to plow ahead is usually not needed by Daugherty—it is simply understood as the executive prerogative.

"I'm not radical, but this is going to, uh ..." he says, as the words trail off. "I think that the good Lord must have had something to do with this because this has been a miracle. All this just didn't happen. I don't know what your—or anyone else who might read this—beliefs are in a higher power. But something other than chance caused all this to happen.

"There have been too many good things. To take pawnshops and turn this into the business that it is, I don't sit here and profess that I am 100 percent responsible for it. I am not an overly religious person, but I don't believe that we crawled up out of the sea and turned into snails and then eventually evolved into human beings either."

This is a rare, weird, awkward moment for the Prince of Pawnbrokers.

No, Jack Daugherty doesn't believe that human beings were once snails.

But, by God, Jack Daugherty really wants you to believe he is on a blessed mission to get cash into the hands of the little man—and make himself wealthy in the process.

***

Before Deep Ellum was reborn as Dallas' nod to nouveau white culture, it was the street of dreams for the city's blacks. A street, through the 1960s, where cold economic facts slammed into the neon-draped seduction offered up by the clubs, eateries and cinema pleasure domes.

It also became Pawnshop Central, a strip that defined perceptions of hockshops as well as the amount of money in thousands of Dallas wallets.

Like it or not, Southland Corp. and its 7-Elevens trace their corporate roots back to Uncle Johnny Green's old icehouse in Oak Cliff. And in 1988, like it or not, Jack Daugherty's lavish office in the Forth Worth Club traces its corporate roots to those dozens of mom-and-pop brokers who fueled the commerce on Dallas' pawn row. It was a stage unto itself, one frequented by an endless audition of actors economically segregated from banks.

Some of the neighborhood's people describe scrambling to buy clothes at Picture's Tailors. At Model's. At Chamber's off the railroad tracks. And sometimes, people made sure they had a pair of Clapp's shoes. Stylish to a fault, sage survivors of days on Deep Ellum—such as City Councilman Al

Lipscomb—knew there was an ulterior motive for taking care of the wardrobe.

"Brother," Lipscomb insists to me in that rattling, rusty-nails-in-a-can voice, "you are going to have a hard time understanding this. But we had good stuff made because we knew that we could pawn it if we needed to. You could redeem those name brands." Honest Joe's. Abe's. Bishop's. Rocky's. Good Old Dave's. They all sang a song of cash-so-fast.

Lipscomb, understated as ever, describes the '50s this way: "We were working at the Adolphus Hotel as dishwashers and pot scrubbers. We were caddying at the Dallas Country Club. But man, the banks had us red-lined, blue-lined, purple-lined, every-kind-of-lined you could think of. So where were we supposed to go to get extra cash? We went to the pawnbroker."

Lipscomb has been thinking a lot about pawnshops recently. About how they may have left Deep Ellum but still live on Martin Luther King Boulevard. And on Jefferson Boulevard—Dallas' second-busiest commercial shopping area outside of downtown in the '50s—where the pawns have resolutely spread as venerable businesses like Bridges Dance Wear have fled.

There are 150 pawnshops in the Dallas area, including an immaculate one next door to an Alexander Julian shop and directly across the street from the highbrow Marty's gourmet and spirits emporium. There, at an unlikely location on Oak Lawn Avenue, the 80-year-old Obi-Wan Kenobi of Dallas pawnbrokers is conducting an impromptu lecture in the aisles.

"Lemme see," Max Wyll says in a voice borrowed from every pool hall and bus station in America. "In Deep Ellum there were the Goldstein brothers. Ruby Goldstein was Honest Joe. Isaac Goldstein was Rocky. Dave Goldstein was Good Old Dave." Wyll meditates for a second: "Harry Meyers was Uncle Jake."

For decades, there were about 50 pawnshops on and around Elm Street. Many of them were owned and operated by a close-knit Jewish confederacy filled with brash guys like Max Wyll. A lot of the pawnbrokers lived in South Dallas around South Boulevard. Many of them graduated from

Forest Avenue, now Madison, High School.

Wyll, who finally abandoned Elm Street last year—his shop was the last one there—started in the business the year after President Herbert Hoover took office. "It was run by Jews back then," he says as he eyeballs a fellow pawnbroker weighing a customer's jewelry. "And it was run by Jews before I started."

In 1930, when the young Wyll got a tip from a buddy that there was work in one of the Elm Street pawnshops, he petitioned Mr. Herm Karl at 2310 Elm. Karl & Winterman was one of the power names on the strip. "Max, you're gonna see a lot of moochers coming in here," Karl advised Wyll. "Take 'em around the corner and buy them lunch, but don't give them any money."

Wyll saw plenty of moochers—raggedy people with kids in tow, all asking for a handout. Wyll made someone else watch the store and he took the beggars around the corner to Al's Cafe, where he staked the Dickensians to sandwiches and coffee.

But when the highways pierced the heart of the neighborhood and the Jews began the exodus from their homes in nearby South Dallas, many of Elm's pawnbrokers hung lease signs in the window. Into the 1970s and 1980s there were fewer and fewer beggars—and still fewer customers. Wyll even saw less and less of the gypsies. They were usually good for regular visits during the year, arriving in packs like big, rolling, Hungarian circus troupes. Wyll learned to fine-tooth his store's inventory after the gypsies piled out his front door.

Finally, in 1987, Wyll's pawnshop was relocated to Oak Lawn. Wyll still opens the door to a handful of regulars who bartered with him over the old Deep Ellum counters. But no one is toting in custom-made clothes. No designer prom gowns or fine shoes from the floor of their closet—the pawns don't take clothing anymore.

Wyll wishes he had kept notes on all the people who gingerly, sheepishly, carried their sacred, memory-laden possessions and gently placed them—as if the inanimate were invested with feelings—before the unemotional pawnbroker.

Each loan-seeker had a different story. The more desperate they were, the more Biblical the epic. This, at least, has remained the same, even if the locations and some of the pawned items might be different.

Wyll is not as cantankerous as the tortured existentialist Rod Steiger played in Sidney Lumet's *The Pawnbroker*, but he has seen just as many things: "I can tell when a guy walks in the door whether he is bull—— or not. I been doing this for more than 50 years. I'll go until I drop."

***

Jack Daugherty is chipper. He has just returned from a week in the United Kingdom. For six straight days, he had six meetings a day, ladling dollops of the pawnshop gospel to shareholders enchanted by Cash America's latest maneuverings.

Daugherty enjoys these business trips to the U.K. He doesn't have to explain himself there as much as in the United States. The first publicly held pawnshop in the world—Harvey & Thompson, founded in 1898—is there.

His foreign investors were equally glad to shake hands and hear from their mammoth Texan, especially about Daugherty's hovering over ColorTyme. "I can only tell you the things I told the stockholders," Daugherty cautiously relents. "It serves the same customer base. It is essentially the same business we are in. It has financing and retail to non-bank customers. It is simply another way to offer the same service."

Though Daugherty and Cash America changed their minds about acquiring ColorTyme—Daugherty has left the door open for "future possibilities"—the move seemed like another attempt to feed an odd financial juggernaut, one already nourished by a simple, two-part economic hypothesis:

If you operate from the premise that there will always be Americans who won't be able to maintain bank accounts, or that there may be an increasing number who will prefer to deal on a cash-only basis, then Daugherty has made a big stride toward hoarding an enormous market.

Some Cash America stores cash payroll checks. And in late 1987, Cash America carried on unfulfilled negotiations to buy ACE Cash Express Inc., a Dallas-based check-cashing company. In other directions, Daugherty oversees three lavish

stores that specialize in reselling high-ticket jewelry items—
the kinds of pieces that Cash America has a hard time hawk-
ing in its pawnshops.

Daugherty won't give much away, but speculation exists
that he is ready to jab his blue-collar-powered arm into lucrative areas such as car loans, money orders and specialty secondhand stores for sporting goods, guns or electronics. When
pressed about possible tie-ins between the 500 ColorTyme
franchises and his 100 pawnshops (the latter are scattered in
Texas, Louisiana, Oklahoma and Tennessee)—Daugherty
coyly says, "We are going to look at other synergies."

One thing is obvious. Daugherty is wholeheartedly
embracing an arena that MBAs, the largest investment houses—and, yes, banks—had run from or never even considered
throughout this century. He is standardizing, computerizing
industries that have played by flexible, personal and very
imprecise rules: Loans given on the weak backs of friendships.
Whims. Mad bargaining. Wailing and pleading. With his goal
of sucking chance out of the pawn business, Jack Daugherty
has moved hockshops off an erratic economic ducking stool
and onto brokers' spreadsheets.

Meanwhile, Daugherty has remained unperturbed by the
tender ethics of an industry that can charge extraordinary
interest rates to people perhaps least likely to afford them.
This is sound, profitable morality, says Daugherty.

"Profitability and education influence most people. That
is the purpose of being an American—to be profitable and successful," advises Daugherty. "We teach our kids that in school.
When we started being successful and profitable, then it got
people's attention. Now Merrill Lynch, now Dean Witter, now
Goldman Sachs—who would not even talk to us—we get letters from all of them."

Daugherty grew up in Irving and never quite earned his
business degree at Texas Tech and Texas Wesleyan. After
school he worked in the private security protection field,
saved $30,000 and used it to start an Irving pawnshop in 1970.
Daugherty dabbled in nightclubs and dry oil holes. The latter
wiped him out of his $300,000 life savings in 1981. He retreat-
ed to ground zero—the pawnshop had remained profitable—

and he simply began acquiring as many as he could.

Daugherty took to dropping into family-run pawns, ones overseen by aging parents with children reluctant to take over an unglamourous business. Daugherty pitched quick offers. In one span of two weeks, he acquired 13 pawns. In a Fort Worth shop, Daugherty came in one morning, kept slinging, and the locks were changed on the front door later that same day.

He also changed the rules. Daugherty's new stores are made to look more like Main Street discount electronic stores than boardinghouses with musty cupboards. The employees are retrained to adhere to uniform loan standards and merchandise pricing. Drug and psychological tests are given.

If someone fails to repay his loan within 90 days, Texas pawns can sell the hocked item: In Daugherty's stores, merchandise that doesn't move is shipped to other stores in the chain. If someone comes in after 90 days, Daugherty says his stores will try to "make a deal with him to get it back."

Regular inventory schedules linking the 100 pawns are introduced. Since pawnbrokers usually only lend a customer 50 to 60 percent of the resale value of the item being hocked, those schedules go a long way toward nourishing the already well-fed profit margins.

Interest rates yo-yo from state to state, as well as according to the number of dollars being borrowed. But Texas, not surprisingly, has some of the highest rates in the nation—78 of Cash America's pawnshops are in Texas (out of almost 700 pawns in the state). If a loan is anywhere up to $96, the "service charge" is as high as 20 percent a month. Interest rates go down from there until you reach 12 percent on loans between $961 and $8,000—$8,000 being the maximum allowable loan offered by pawnshops.

There are no bad loans: Cash America's outstanding loans yield 210 percent annually, while the company has sometimes paid roughly 9 percent for its own borrowed money. Most people pay back their loan within 45 days, though 30 percent of Daugherty's customers default on their loans and lose their property.

Still, in the end, there are some things all these good figures can't make disappear. Pawns will probably always wallow in a vat of sleazy images, especially smeared by the one firm belief that pawnshops are the first stop for the people who just left your back door with your new color TV.

Daugherty points to a 1985 study at his stores indicating that out of 135,000 transactions only 35 pieces of merchandise were not legitimate. And by law, pawnbrokers must submit daily itemized reports on their merchandise to police.

The Dallas Police Department has an eight-man pawnshop detail. Now, City Councilman Lipscomb wants video cameras installed in pawnshops to further discourage thieves from cashing in on hot items. This is the kind of bad public relations that makes Daugherty suffer severe mood swings.

"Let me talk to you about that," he begins. "You are already required to have a positive identification. A positive ID is a driver's license or a military ID card with a picture on it, or, as an alternative, a thumbprint. A camera in a store is nothing more than just another picture. It is a moot point."

Daugherty begins warming up his philosophical fife and drum corps: "All of Cash America's customers, all pawn customers, are citizens of the United States. Just as you and I are citizens of the United States. They are all non-bank customers. To treat them differently is about as unconstitutional as you can get," he orates. "To treat someone differently who makes $14,000 a year than you do someone who makes $100,000 a year goes against the thrust of what the whole country is about."

When Daugherty took Cash America public in 1987— with 35 pawnshops—he raised $15.5 million. Shortly after the initial public offering, Cash America completed a successful $37.5 million acquisition of the 47-store Waco-based Big State chain of pawnshops. In a wobbly Texas economy, he partially funded the move through a private offering. More letters began arriving.

> *Dear Sir:*
> *We have watched the progress of your company since listing and note the extremely good financial results achieved ... We have recently investigated the opportunities in the pawnbroking industry in Australia ... the purpose of this letter is to bring this to your*

attention and, moreover, to explore the possibility of joining with
you.

Daugherty's office is littered with other offers from Canada, Germany, Austria, Argentina and France. And there are "investment research" reports issued by investment houses such as Eppler, Guerin & Turner Inc.:

"We believe Cash America represents an exciting growth company operating in a sector of the financial service industry that is, in our opinion, almost completely unknown in the investment community, the pawnshop industry. Unlike most financial service companies, PWN's fortunes are not dictated by the cost of money or by interest rate levels. ... Since the industry is very fragmented, there is little information regarding the typical pawnshop customer.

"He is not the unsavory character portrayed on television programs or in the news media. Defining the customer base is somewhat difficult; those people without a checking account or any financial institution relationship constitutes a good categorial description. We believe 20 percent of the population falls into this category."

More prospective customers may be close at hand. Maybe a bank collapse or two away. Texas institutions have continued to tumble all year, and it's an easy trick to drum up Malthusians convinced that the FDIC, the FSLIC and even the Social Security system are all going to hell. There are plenty out there who just lapsed into nightmarish naps after reading make-room-for-the-apocalypse chapters in *The Great Depression of 1990* by Dallas' Ravi Batra.

Meanwhile, Daugherty's business continues to be about cash and reality. It is not certificates of deposit or money market accounts. It is your antique necklace, your VCR, your child's clarinet, your school ring. Real things—in paranoid times—that you can wrap your warm-blooded hands around. It is not the paper world of banks.

Daugherty doesn't worry about the banks so much as have contempt for them: "We work with MBank here in Fort Worth. It has taken us all of the years we have been in business to educate them. And the reason we stick with them is that they are probably the only bank in the United States that understands what we are doing. I don't want to go through that process again."

Daugherty has a word for most inner-city banks. We can't use that word.

"Now these [banks] here in town that loan money here on these giant real estate and oil deals. They are all going busted. But these small banks who stuck to loaning money to guys with 100 heads of hogs and 50 acres of wheat—they know these guys are not going anywhere. ... Banks have always stuck the finger at us and said shame on you."

The week the massive MCorp bank holding company finally admits it needs help. Daugherty's voice is filled with a knowing somberness. "Seems it lasted longer," he says of MCorp. He knew the company was going to stagger: "I've just been wondering when."

Daugherty has a habit of abruptly interrupting a conversation with a question, a question leading up to a sermon:

"Operating on a cash basis is not too stupid. You have an accountant?" he suddenly demands. "Look here. Here is my accountant," he says. Daugherty is slipping into his imitation of the thousands of people he deals with who never handle checks. He digs into his pocket.

"I reach in," he says, "and I know exactly where I stand every time."

As though it's the most pure talisman since Moses' stones, Daugherty is waving a rectangular, glittering, gold money clip that's taking a big pouty bite into a healthy clump of American cash.

Part IV
Mortgaging Your Future:
Home-Loan Rip-Offs

Just before credits roll in the movie "Tin Men," a couple of early '60s aluminum-siding salesmen commiserate about losing their home-improvement licenses to a city commission that wants to stop con men who steal the equity in people's homes through shoddy work financed by rip-off mortgages. "You wanna know what our big crime is?" the tin man played by Richard Dreyfuss says. "We're nickel-and-dime guys, just small-time hustlers who got caught because we're hustling nickels and dimes."

In real life, decades later, tin men are still at work. But mortgage rip-offs are no longer nickel-and-dime stuff. Mortgage companies are raking in billions via salesmen who talk homeowners into signing high-interest loans to repair aging rowhouses, pay off medical bills or stave off foreclosure. These borrowers are often black, elderly, working or retired people who have struggled for decades to buy their homes.

Many banks have profited by bankrolling or owning these lenders. Citibank purchased loans for more than a decade from the Dartmouth Plan, a national lender accused of cheating 27,000 borrowers in New York and Connecticut alone. Citibank paid $250,000 to settle a New York attorney general's lawsuit over its ties to Dartmouth. Fleet Financial Group, New England's biggest bank, ended up pledging at least $284 million to end lawsuits and government investigations of its Atlanta-based mortgage subsidiary.

Loan Scams

Michael Hudson,
APF Reporter, **Alicia Patterson Foundation, 1992**

Some days it seems like the phone at Annie Ruth Bennett's house in southwest Atlanta won't ever stop ringing. The callers want to sell her storm windows, debt-consolidation loans, burial plots. Her attorney says it's all a scheme: They want to steal a piece of her home by getting her to take out a loan against its value.

But now she knows better. She and her husband Frank, 73, are already struggling to pay $469 a month of their tiny incomes to cover a loan from Fleet Finance, a giant national mortgage company. The Bennetts say they took out the loan after a home-repair contractor knocked on their door and offered to fix up their small frame house. He arranged an 18.5-percent second mortgage. Then he took nearly $10,000 to pay himself—for work that an appraiser later valued at $1,245.

Now a sheet of plastic covers a gaping hole where the drop-ceiling the contractor installed in their living room fell in. The Bennetts say they can't afford to buy shoes anymore, let alone fix the damage.

William Brennan, Jr., their Legal Aid attorney, charges that the Bennetts were victims of a new twist on an old scam—one that has been given new life by mainstream banks hungry for profits. Advocates for the poor claim that respectable banks and savings and loans are using home-repair contractors and second-mortgage companies as front operations to prey on the poor.

The Bennetts' loan was made by Home Equity Centers, of Marietta, Georgia, which in turn sold it to Fleet Finance. Fleet is an Atlanta-based subsidiary of Fleet Financial Group, New England's largest bank. Court records show Fleet Finance has had connections with Home Equity Centers dating back to a 1983 brokers' agreement and a 1985 business loan it made to the smaller company. From 1985 to early 1991, Fleet purchased more than 90 percent of the loans made by Home Equity Centers in Atlanta's DeKalb County. Attorneys for homeowners in Atlanta have filed a lawsuit accusing the two companies of taking their property "by deceitful means and artful practices." Both deny any wrongdoing.

"Tin men" peddling shady home-repair loans have been around for decades, but they're no longer just small-time operators. They are part of a national epidemic of second-mortgage abuses. Interviews with Legal Aid attorneys, private lawyers and attorney general offices across the nation show that hundreds of thousands of low-income homeowners have been victimized in the past decade. Many have lost their homes outright. Others have had the equity sucked out of their property.

Thanks to the free-wheeling brand of capitalism that emerged during the Reagan era and lax regulation by state and federal governments, home equity ripoffs have become big business: well-organized, demographically targeted and nationally franchised.

Tin men and mortgage brokers prowl minority neighborhoods and offer poor, working-class or elderly homeowners loans at interest rates that often reach 20 percent a year. Tacked-on service fees raise the price of borrowing even higher.

The banking industry makes this sort of lending possible by starving low-income and minority neighborhoods of mainstream credit. Borrowers in these neighborhoods have nowhere to turn except to high-interest mortgage companies. Meanwhile, some banks and savings and loans have profited from these same second-mortgage companies' questionable practices by lending them money for operating expenses or by purchasing the loan contracts after they're signed.

In Boston, for example, another subsidiary of Fleet Financial Group extended a $7.5 million line of credit to one of the city's most notorious second-mortgage lenders, Resource Financial Group. The company is now bankrupt and the state has charged it with fraud. A study by Union Neighborhood Assistance Corp., a Boston community group, found that more than 80 percent of the homeowners who took out mortgages from Resource either lost their homes or were facing foreclosure. Better than 90 percent of the loans were in minority neighborhoods where, studies have shown, mainstream banks seldom loan money.

The second-mortgage scandal has taken on added urgency in the aftermath of this spring's riots in Los Angeles. After a long period of neglect, news outlets and government officials have been forced to look at the economic exploitation of America's inner cities.

South Central Los Angeles, which was at the center of the unrest that claimed 60 lives, has been one of the most fertile grounds in the nation for home-equity fraud. Lawyers say that con artists cruise South Central neighborhoods, spot likely houses, and then use car phones to call their offices, which tap into real estate databases to see whether the homeowner is a promising mark. Troy Smith, a Legal Aid lawyer in Los Angeles who specializes in housing cases, says con artists often pump their cash flow by using the house they've stolen as collateral for more bank loans. Too often, the house sits vacant until it is taken over by gangs and drug dealers who terrorize the neighborhood. Smith believes tens of thousands of homeowners have been victims of equity fraud throughout the city's minority neighborhoods.

The story is much the same in Atlanta, which also endured rioting this spring. Second mortgage scams are so bad there that the DeKalb County government has funded a Home Defense Office. Brennan, who heads the program, started representing poor people as a Legal Aid lawyer in Atlanta in 1968. Back then, his biggest worry was making sure his clients weren't unfairly denied public housing or welfare. Sure, there were corner grocers who price-gouged in poor neighborhoods, slippery door-to-door salesman and, of course, tin men. The poor have always paid more for goods and services. But, Brennan contends, businesses that prey on the poor simply weren't as organized and vicious as they are today.

During the Reagan era, Brennan says, blaming the poor for their problems became fashionable again at the same time that the free-enterprise ethic was reinvigorated. Profiting from low-income people's misfortunes suddenly became more acceptable—even if it meant taking the homes of long-time residents who have provided stability to deteriorating neighborhoods. In Los Angeles, Smith sees that attitude all the time: "I can't tell you how many times I've gone into court with a deal that was fraudulent and the judge says: It's just business. It was a business deal that your client didn't get the best of."

In Atlanta, Brennan says that scam artists see older black homeowners as easy marks because they are usually less educated and financially unsophisticated. These homeowners often have large chunks of equity built up in their homes, because they've spent decades paying their house notes and because real estate values have inflated rapidly in the past two decades. That equity, Brennan says, makes a tantalizing target for loan brokers, tin men, second-mortgage companies and banks.

"It's like finding a ten-dollar bill in the street and saying: This is mine, I'm gonna take it. Their attitude is: It's there for the taking."

One day recently, Brennan had office visits from three older black women who came in for wills and other legal work not related to home-equity loans.

As an experiment, he asked each if they owned their homes. All three said yes.

Were the houses paid for, or almost paid for? They were.

Were they getting calls from people who wanted to loan them money on their houses?

"All three of them, we got the same answer: I get calls every day of the week, Monday through Friday, two and three times a day."

In their defense, Fleet and other banks say the home-repair and second-mortgage dealers they do business with are completely separate companies. There may have been abuses in a few cases, bankers say, but they had no way of knowing. "These people may be poor and illiterate, but no one puts a gun to their head and tells them to sign," Fleet Financial Group vice president Robert W. Lougee told the *Boston Globe*. "This idea that Fleet should regulate the world is preposterous." Fleet and two other big Massachusetts banks, Baybanks and Shawmut, have reached settlements with the state promising to put up $35 million to repay victims of home equity scams. The money also will be used to make loans to first-time home buyers.

Second mortgages are an American growth industry. Duff and Phelps Credit Rating Company says home equity lending jumped from $1 billion in 1982 to $100 billion in 1988.

The "secondary market" for second mortgages—where banks buy home-equity loan contracts from other lenders—was virtually non-existent when the Federal National Mortgage Association, a quasi-government agency, started buying them in the early 1980s. Since then, second-mortgage speculation has boomed.

Surveys by the Consumer Bankers Association show that the number of big banks buying home equity loans on the secondary market grew from 12.5 percent in 1990 to 20.9 percent in 1991. Fleet Finance, for example, said last year that about 60 percent of its 71,000 mortgages had been purchased from other lenders. The company made profits of $60 million in 1990.

The vast majority of equity loans involve middle- to upper-income borrowers. It's unfair to suggest that every tin man or second-mortgage company is a fraud, or that every bank that buys second mortgages from them is exploiting poor people. But a sample of court cases across the country indicates that second-mortgage abuses are widespread.

• In Chicago, Community Bank of Greater Peoria agreed in 1991 to pay as much as $4 million to settle a class-action lawsuit involving more than 6,275 homeowners. The borrowers said they were victimized by deceptive loans arranged by 40 tin men who had working relationships with the bank.

The bank denied working with shady contractors but acknowledged some "technical violations."

• In New York, the attorney general charged a mortgage company named Dartmouth Plan in 1990 with defrauding as many as 20,000 borrowers and then siphoning $25 million out of the corporation via a phony employee stock plan. The state also sued a dozen banks that bought mortgages from the company.

Dartmouth has agreed to pay as much as $4 million to settle a criminal investigation of fraud charges involving 7,000 homeowners in Connecticut. State officials there said the company made mortgages in at least 38 states before going out of business in 1990.

To increase its volume, Dartmouth dangled the offer of trips to Hawaii, Monte Carlo, Rome and Spain as incentives to sales people who brought in lots of loans or got customers to sign up for high interest rates.

• In Virginia, Landbank Equity and Freedlander Inc. operated as giant fraud schemes—stealing from borrowers and investors alike—until the companies' top executives were arrested and put in prison. Landbank made 10,000 loans in five states. Freedlander, once the nation's fourth largest mortgage company, expanded into 33 states and made 37,000 loans totaling $675 million before its collapse in 1988.

• In Alabama, three juries hit Union Mortgage of Dallas with more than $57 million in fraud verdicts in 1991. In one case, five families won $45 million after being swindled by a tin man that the company had recruited despite a record of 14 lawsuits, liens and court judgments against him. Attorneys for the victims say Union made 40,000 predatory loans across the United States. A former Union branch manager in Alabama testified that there's a catch-phrase sometimes used in the industry to describe how borrowers can be hoodwinked with fast talk and confusing paperwork: "Cash out the deal before the customer comes out from under the ether."

The deregulation of the mortgage industry set the stage for second-mortgage scams against these homeowners in much the same way that deregulation of savings and loans created the S&L scandal. Since the late 1970s, federal and state lawmakers have struck down almost all limits on second-mortgage interest charges or created loopholes that made it easy for creative lenders to skirt usury laws.

At the same time, the federal government does nothing to regulate second-mortgage companies. It has left responsibility for policing the industry with the states, many of which take a hands-off approach. In Massachusetts, for example, second-mortgage companies have generally been able to charge whatever interest rate they want—as long as they notify the state attorney general's office if they intend to charge 20 percent or more.

Brennan traces the genesis of large-scale equity ripoffs in Georgia to 1983—when the state legislature wiped out all laws limiting mortgage interest except for a 1908 loan-sharking law. It limits interest on loans to 5 percent *per month*.

In Pennsylvania, one finance company used a home mortgage loophole to avoid interest caps on used-car loans. The company was free to charge whatever rate it wanted by requiring that borrowers secure their loans against their cars *and* their homes (or the homes of co-signers). The company charged annual rates as high as 41 percent. According to testimony in a lawsuit, one down-on-his-luck borrower who tried to return his car was told: "We don't want your car; We want your aunt's house." The company secured one loan, on a $3,500 Buick, against the borrower's household goods, his house, and his mother-in-law's house.

More than a dozen states do not regulate second-mortgage lenders at all. In Georgia, for example, you have to have a license to be a hairdresser, but not to work as a mortgage broker.

At the same time, housing activists say, federal officials have been halfhearted in enforcing fair lending laws that require that banks make an effort to do business in low-income and minority neighborhoods. Study after study has shown that U.S. banks and S&Ls are reluctant to loan cash in minority neighborhoods. In 1988, a Pulitzer Prize-winning series by the *Atlanta Journal and Constitution* found that whites in Atlanta receive five times as many home loans from mainstream lenders as blacks with similar incomes.

Frank and Annie Ruth Bennett have owned their house on a tree-lined street in Atlanta since 1969. Over the past decade, they've made several attempts to fix it up. Each time, they've fallen a little more into debt to second-mortgage companies. Even so, they still had managed to hang onto more than half the equity in the house, which is worth nearly $50,000.

Now, with a debt of around $28,000 to Fleet plus about $7,000 left on their original house note, most of the value in their property belongs to someone else. His Social Security check and her wages as a cafeteria worker for Delta Airlines aren't enough to keep up. They have fallen behind and have had to pay delinquency charges to Fleet. "It's not just tight, I'm telling you," Annie Ruth Bennett said.

She said that when a man called recently trying to sell her storm windows, she told him: "When I get ready, I'll get in touch with you." He called again, and she put him off again. Then he had a woman—his wife or secretary Bennett guessed—call yet again.

"I just tell them I'm sleepy and I don't feel like talking," Bennett said. "I'm not signing no papers. I've learned my lesson."

Editor's Epilogue

Fleet Financial Group announced in early 1996 that it was putting Fleet Finance up for sale. It said the decision had to do with the earlier allegations against the company.

Company's Success
Fires Up Wall Street

Michael Hudson,
The Roanoke (Virginia) *Times*, **Dec. 11, 1994**

United Companies Financial Corp. likes to compare itself to "fast food before Ray Kroc." United Companies executives believe they're poised—like McDonalds in the 1950s—to take over a huge, growing market.

The Louisiana-based company makes loans to people who can't qualify for mortgages from banks or savings and loans. With the help of funding from Wall Street investors, United Companies has captured a growing share of a credit market that financial analysts say could reach $100 billion a year.

"There are 11,000 banks in the country and maybe 2,000 thrifts," United Companies president J. Terrell Brown told a trade publication, *The American Banker.* "If each one of their branches turns down one loan a week, then it's a lot of small numbers that all of a sudden get big. And that's what really fires me up."

In little more than two years, the lender has expanded from 17 states to 34, and its loan production has grown from $301 million to a projected $900 million this year. All this has fired Wall Street up—United Companies stock price shot up 340 percent last year, and it has become known as one of America's hottest stock buys.

Other people are fired up about United Companies too—but for different reasons.

Freda Spears and her husband got a loan from United Companies to buy a used mobile home to put on a plot of land they owned in Bedford County, Virginia.

They had bad marks on their credit history coming into the deal, so they knew it would be difficult to get a bank loan. But she says United Companies' newspaper ad "sounded so rosy: No matter how bad your credit is, you can get a loan."

Spears was pleased to get the credit, and they later refinanced and increased their debt with United Companies to just under $19,000.

But she says she now realizes the interest rate—19.85 percent on the second loan—was more than she could afford. And she complains the company added $1,323 worth of credit insurance she didn't want in the loan.

When an injury put her husband out of work and unpaid bills piled up, the couple asked for an extension from United Companies. "They wouldn't consider it whatsoever," she says.

In the end, the family saved the trailer and land by filing for bankruptcy. Their attorney worked out a court-ordered plan that reduced their interest rate and stretched out their payments.

Spears wishes she'd gone elsewhere: "I think finance companies that charge outrageous rates like that—people should be aware of the way they do," Spears says. "There's probably a lot of people like us who didn't know.... My advice would be to shop around—and not deal with United Companies at all."

At least a few other borrowers agree. In Alabama, one couple won a $500,000 jury verdict over an alleged home-improvement scam and the company also agreed to pay $4.45 million to settle a class-action lawsuit. It faces more lawsuits in Alabama and Georgia.

United Companies officials deny breaking the law in any of these cases. They say the rates they charge are fair, and that borrowers sign a disclosure form when they purchase credit insurance with their loans. United Companies says it takes more risks than banks, because their customers have shakier credit records, and sometimes must foreclose to recover the money it lent out.

"What we do in our business is make credit available to folks who really need it," spokesman Louis Resweber says. "We've been in business for half a century—and we've received numerous awards for the type of business we do. If you look at the hundreds of thousands of loans we make, I don't think you're going to see anything other than a track record that is commendable and exemplary."

Resweber notes that the company has earned complimentary write-ups in the *New York Times*, *Fortune* and other major publications.

United Companies has drawn the ire of some community activists, however, because of the allegations in the lawsuits—and because of the way Wall Street investors have fueled its growth.

"United Companies has refined the art of predatory lending and in some ways has become the epitome," says Marty Leary, a research analyst with the Hotel Employees and Restaurant Employees International Union who has studied high-cost mortgage lenders. "They have figured out a way to tap virtually unlimited resources from Wall Street."

United Companies is a leading example of how the "nonconforming" mortgage market—higher interest loans to people with bad credit or low incomes—has become an extremely profitable business. The first six months of this year, the company pulled in $28.4 million in after-tax profits on $172.5 million in revenues.

United Companies began in 1946. Its late founder, Lloyd F. Collette, swore by this motto: "Mama might let some other payments slide, but she's going to be sure to pay that house note first."

His successors still follow that maxim, according to *The American Banker*. But the company didn't reach critical mass until 1992, when it jumped into the "mortgage-backed" securities market. Mortgage-backed securities are a 1980s investment wrinkle that allows lenders to increase their cash flow by selling bonds backed by the income from their mortgages.

Critics contend mortgage-backed securities have an undesirable side effect: They've opened up a pool of money for predatory lenders. Fleet Financial Group, New England's largest bank, used these securities to expand its business in "nonconforming" mortgages—until lawsuits and government investigations forced the lender out of the market.

Leary, the union financial researcher, says bond underwriters and other key Wall Street players have given their blessing to mortgage-backed securities deals arranged by United Companies and other lenders that seek out disadvantaged borrowers. He argues that investors get the best of all possible worlds—low risks, high returns—because these borrowers pay a "poverty tax" of higher fees and interest rates that far outstrip any risks created by their lower incomes or flawed credit record.

Resweber, the company spokesman, said United Companies actually charges lower rates than most other non-bank mortgage lenders that serve the same pool of borrowers. Last year United Companies charged an average interest rate of just under 12 percent, compared to the national average of between 6 percent and 7 percent charged by banks and S&Ls. United Companies also charge upfront fees of 7 percent, compared to a national average of 1.75 percent on conventional mortgages.

Its loans are a bit more likely to have late payments or get written off as bad debts than conventional bank loans, company president Brown told *The American Banker*, "but hopefully we priced our risk adequately."

Resweber says the company's aim is to help borrowers "repair their credit history and position themselves to qualify for conventional credit as quickly as possible."

As an example of the company's community spirit, Resweber points to the case of a Pensacola, Florida, man it saved from homelessness. United Companies sold John Jones—a retired truck driver who had been evicted from his rental home—a house for just $57 a month for 10 years. Its employees also organized a clean-up and repair day to whip the house into shape. "I can't tell you how much this means to me," Jones said. "Nothing ever happened like this before in my life."

Some other customers have been less appreciative of United Companies:

• In 1991, the Alabama Supreme Court upheld a $500,000 jury verdict against the company. The justices agreed with the jury that the company was guilty of fraud and breach of contract against a couple who had borrowed $12,000 for home repairs.

According to testimony, Abram Brown and Rosie Holcombe already had someone to do the work, but United Companies said it would make the loan only if it picked the contractor. The contractor never finished the work, but the loan officer talked them into paying anyway, promising he'd make sure the work was done. It wasn't, and a county judge said the couple was forced to "live in deplorable conditions for months and months"—in a kitchen without water, rooms without walls and a bathroom with only a hole in the floor instead of a toilet.

United Companies argued there was no proof the loan agent intended to defraud the couple, and that there was no breach of contract because the loan officer's promises were never put into writing.

• In 1993, the company settled a lawsuit in Tampa, Florida, charging that it had violated federal truth-in-lending rules on a home-repair loan. Andres and Paula Guajardo claimed the lender had charged them for a $1,300 broker's fee that it didn't deserve—because the loan had been arranged by a subsidiary, United Companies Mortgage of Florida, and not by an independent broker.

• That same year, United Companies company agreed to pay $4.45 million to settle a lawsuit charging it with over-charging 1,000 to 1,500 working-class borrowers in rural Alabama.

The borrowers' lawyers say the company charged them as much as 20 percent in upfront finance fees—even though state law limited such fees to 5 percent. According to expert testimony, one customer paid the equivalent of an annual interest rate of 61 percent.

Cathy Lucrezi, a lawyer with Florida Rural Legal Services, says there's "some nugget of truth" to the company's argument that it provides a service by lending money to people when they really need it. But the problem is that the cash comes "with outrageous strings attached" at a time when they're most desperate and vulnerable.

Company spokesman Resweber counters that if the lender mistreated its customers, "we wouldn't have the referral rate that we do. We wouldn't have the repeat business rate that we do."

He said the complaints are isolated cases—representing a handful of loans compared to the 58,000 mortgages United Companies has outstanding.

"With any organization," he says, "there are are lot of things happening out there."

Part V
Shattered Dreams:
New Homes, Unhappy Home Owners

The dream of owning a home can also be a trap. Many companies that build homes for disadvantaged consumers gouge them via second-rate construction or financing scams. Fleet Finance, the Atlanta-based lender accused of predatory home-equity lending, also drew fire for buying hundreds of mortgages from real-estate developers accused of cheating new home buyers with bad credit records. In the 1980s, Florida's General Development Corp. lured more than 100,000 families into buying lots or homes that were inflated by as much as 100 percent over their actual value. Companies hustling Florida dream homes to unsophisticated consumers in the Northeast have been around for decades. What makes the GDC case particularly interesting is that its sales program was devised under the watchful eye of its lawyers at Cravath, Swaine & Moore, perhaps the richest law firm in America. Another major homebuilder, Jim Walter Corp., has been dogged for more than two decades by allegations that it rips off working-class consumers, many of them black or Hispanic families.

A Firm Blessing

Attorneys from Cravath found a developer's plan lawful. A jury disagreed.

Rita Henley Jensen,
National Law Journal, **August 24, 1992**

MIAMI—This is the story of the houses that Cravath, Swaine & Moore helped build. And the tale of the legal architecture behind these structures provides a rare insight into the advice the patrician New York law firm gave to a significant client—a major Florida home developer—and the disastrous results for most everyone concerned.

One of these houses can be reached by driving three-and-a-half hours due north of Miami, turning west off Interstate 95, left again through a subdivision and eventually negotiating a road dotted with potholes wider than a car. The tiny, two-bedroom, one-and-a-half bath ranch, and a similar one next door, sit isolated on Port Malabar, Florida's Upland Avenue, amid the pines and scrub palmettos of inland central Florida, about a mile from the nearest schools and stores.

This house, owned by a pair of Jamaican immigrant sisters, is one of more than 10,000 homes built by one of Florida's largest developers, General Development Corp., from 1983 to 1989. The details surrounding its sale, and the sale of others like it, were important evidence in helping federal prosecutors convict four of GDC's officers Aug. 5 of fraud or conspiracy.

The advice Cravath gave its client, GDC, during those years—that its lot and home sales operations were beyond reproach—was key to the company's continuing operations, testimony given during the fraud and conspiracy trial makes clear.

Cravath had served as counsel to its parent company, City Investing Co., since the 1970s, until GDC was spun off to shareholders in 1985. Subsequently, Cravath served as GDC's corporate counsel, and in 1987 it became chief litigation counsel. The chairman of the board, David F. Brown, was a former

Cravath associate; Cravath partner David G. Ormsby was the secretary to the board from 1985 through 1988; and in 1988, Cravath attorney Gregory Flemming became the vice president/law and also served as board secretary. In fact, in 1989, Cravath received fees from GDC of about $5 million—1.4 percent of the firm's total revenues of $357 million.

(Cravath faces a class action filed in New Jersey federal court, in part for its role in what the plaintiffs charge are transactions between GDC and its parent that left the developer cash-poor and heavily in debt.)

And for Cravath litigator Paul M. Dodyk, 54, GDC was enormously important. During the critical years of 1987 through 1989—during a grand jury investigation and at a time when homeowners were filing lawsuits against GDC by the handfuls—the developer was one of Mr. Dodyk's four largest accounts, and in 1989 it was his largest, according to trial testimony.

Cravath, one of the most profitable law firms in the nation, if not the world, traces its roots back to 1819. It has eschewed geographic expansion, and its only office outside New York is an eight-lawyer presence in London. With 70 partners and 250 associates, it is the inventor of the so-called Cravath system of firm management, named after the late Paul D. Cravath. It includes such modern-day fixtures as high associate-partner ratios, long apprenticeships of salaried associates, few lateral hires and extensive training of associates by partners.

Firm Chairman Samuel C. Butler declined to comment on the case.

**

During the recent nine-month-long trial of the four ex-officers of GDC, Cravath's name was so frequently invoked that the firm itself became an offstage presence. Mr. Dodyk's testimony was considered so key to the litigation that the day before his scheduled July 17 testimony, U.S. District Judge Lenore C. Nesbitt openly expressed her delight that Mr. Dodyk finally would be on the witness stand.

The stakes were high by then. Mr. Brown and three other GDC officers had been charged with conspiracy and 20 counts each of mail fraud and inducing others to travel as part of the scheme, which lasted from 1983 to 1989. Mr. Dodyk was the last defense witness to be called, after 114 trial days and 24,280 pages of testimony.

The future of four GDC officers was up for grabs. If Mr. Dodyk failed to convince the jury that his client's sales practices were "legal and moral" as he would claim, the four could face long prison terms, if Judge Nesbitt remained true to her word.

In 1990, Mr. Brown and the company president, Robert F. Ehrling, had agreed to plead guilty to a single pre-Sentencing Guidelines conspiracy count. However, Judge Nesbitt had refused to approve the pleas. The one-count plea limited her to meting out a maximum sentence of five years, and she wanted more "flexibility," she said at the time. Rather than agree to serve longer sentences, the two opted for trial, and subsequently the grand jury indicted them, plus two other GDC officers. If Mr. Dodyk could convince the jury that the four could legitimately claim the reliance-on-counsel defense, they might go free and the enormous gamble of going to trial would pay off.

It was an occasion of immense personal importance to Mr. Dodyk as well. For this was the first opportunity Mr. Dodyk had to explain to a jury how strongly he believed his clients had done nothing wrong. Offering courtroom support were Cravath partner Ronald S. Rolfe, an associate and two summer clerks, and his wife.

The other litigation concerning GDC's sales practices had been settled without trial. As the result of a related probe, the company itself pleaded guilty to one count of conspiring to defraud customers in 1990, shortly before it filed for bankruptcy. As part of its settlement with the government, the company agreed to pay up to $150 million in restitution. GDC also settled 104 individual suits, for a total of $4 million, brought by two Florida plaintiffs' attorneys, Douglas S. Lyons and Rick Bennett, and will settle with about 100,000 additional home buyers and lot purchasers as part of its reorganization plan. Adding to the stakes, the fees for the defense team, led by the current president of the American College of Trial

Lawyers, Robert B. Fiske Jr. of New York's Davis Polk & Wardwell, had mounted to more than $10 million.

Was There a House?

One critical moment came during Mr. Dodyk's testimony, when he was asked by Asst. U.S. Attorney Norman Moskowitz to comment on the appraisal for the Upland Avenue house. His answers were precise and technically correct, but he seemed unable to state the obvious, to see the forest for the trees. Such appraisals, as Mr. Dodyk knew, were critical to the government's fraud claims because the appraisers compared the GDC prices only to those of other houses built by GDC, not the substantially lower prices of houses built by local contractors.

Mr. Dodyk, looking more like a Congregational minister in his tropical-weight tan suit and ordinary glasses than a Wall Street lawyer, readily agreed that the appraisal was typical of those used by GDC's financing arm when it was arranging mortgages for the properties it sold.

Mr. Moskowitz asked Mr. Dodyk to turn to the final page of the appraisal, upon which two photos of the "subject property" were pasted. He asked him if they were of a house. No house appeared in the foreground of either, but Mr. Dodyk seemed to have trouble admitting that.

Of the top photograph, which features an empty lot front and center and a partially constructed house off to the left and in the rear, Mr. Dodyk said: "I can't really tell whether that house in the top photograph is the one which is intended to be valued or not. It's not completed. ... And the front part of the picture doesn't have a house in it," Mr. Dodyk said.

Q. "That house is kind of the background, right?"

A. "Right."

Q. "In the foreground of the picture, it's just dirt, right?"

A. "Right."

Q. "And the picture below that, there's no house, there is just a road, right, and a car?"

After a pause, Mr. Dodyk answered: "Well, there is a house on the right-hand side of the road." After another pause, he added, "But I don't know whether that's the house they are talking about or not."

***

It wasn't. The house in question had yet to be built on Upland Avenue in Port Malabar in 1984 when two sisters, nurses from the New York borough of Queens, signed a contract with GDC agreeing to purchase it for $75,330 after GDC constructed it.

One of the sisters, Florencia Allen, now 72, works part-time to help pay her mortgage. She was one of 20 prosecution witnesses called to illustrate GDC sales practices.

The two sisters, both immigrants from Jamaica, purchased a lot in the 1970s from another developer in the Silver Springs area for $5,000. According to Ms. Allen's testimony, in the 1980s, GDC took over the Silver Springs development. Soon GDC began sending the sisters brochures, leaflets, and pamphlets. GDC sales representatives started calling Ms. Allen and her sister at work and at home and telling them: "It's time now, because later they will be going up," Ms. Allen testified.

A salesman came to Ms. Allen's Queens home Aug. 27, 1984, and explained to the sisters that the lot they owned could not be sold, but that they could trade it in on a house. And if they did not intend to move down to Florida right away, they could rent it and "make some money off of it," Ms. Allen testified, "and most likely pay our mortgage." The salesman estimated that the rent would come to between $500 and $600 per month.

The salesman showed the sisters a brochure featuring comfortable homes and beaches. Port Malabar would be developed shortly, the salesman promised, with schools, clinics and hospitals. All this could be had for a "reasonable" price, she testified.

A week later, Ms. Allen and her sister were winging their way toward Florida at GDC's expense on what the company referred to as its "Southward Ho" trip. Prospects were discouraged from renting cars and encouraged to rely on GDC for transportation.

Dinner and a Pitch

True to form, the two sisters were met at the airport by a salesman; he drove them to their hotel, and the salesman and his spouse joined them for dinner. The dinner conversation centered on how good the living was in Florida. The next day, the salesman drove them around, looking at GDC houses, which they did not like because they were too small. The salesman showed them a house floor plan that he said would be bigger than the ones they looked at. And he assured them they could rent it using Florida Home Finders Inc. for $500 a month.

"He impressed us that it would be all right, and we would rent it and the rent would pay our mortgage," Ms. Allen testified.

The next day they signed a contract and were driven to the airport by the salesman. They agreed to pay a total of $75,330—$53,490 for the house, about $4,000 in site preparation costs and an appraisal fee of $155—and were given a purchase credit equal to $17,495, the value of the lot the sisters owned. The sisters were assured they would not need an attorney at the closing.

The purchase was made possible by the home developer's financing arm, GDV Financial Corp., which arranged a $56,000 variable-rate mortgage. The appraisal stated that the mortgage had a 74.34 percent loan-to-value ratio—in line with the industry standard that home mortgages should be for no more than 75 percent of the market value.

Shortly after they bought it, Ms. Allen was told by an agent for Florida Home Finders that the house could not be rented right away and the potential rent was "as far as the east is from the west"—only $375 a month, Ms. Allen testified. The sisters expressed an interest in selling. GDC representatives advised them to be patient until the market improved.

"So we try to hold on, but as time went on, we were spending so much money on that house for repairs and everything else that I was crying every day," Ms. Allen testified. The sisters' mortgage payment was $661 a month; the rent—before costs and Home Finders' 10 percent commission—was never more than $400 a month, and frequently less.

They again decided to sell, and Ms. Allen called a realtor not connected to GDC. She learned that three-bedroom homes in the area were selling for as low as $35,000 and as high as

$48,000. She called GDC; she was told the current selling price was $42,000—$33,330 less than the purchase price and $14,000 less than their mortgage.

During cross, Ms. Allen admitted that she had not read many of the documents she had signed. "We were so naive," she said at one point.

***

Ms. Allen's testimony contains the elements of many of the prosecution's charges against GDC: That the lot trade-in program was part of a scheme to mislead customers; that the advertisement the sales staff showed customers gave the impression that the values of the homes were going up; that the Southward Ho trips were designed to control the customers and prevent them from learning that the houses were priced above value and to mislead customers about the rental market; that the company financed the purchases, again, to prevent the discovery that there was a wide disparity between the houses' true value and their price; and that the skewed appraisals furthered the ruse by creating the impression of a normal transaction. The prosecution also charged that GDC targeted so-called ethnic markets composed of recent immigrants.

Cravath's representation preceded Ms. Allen's transactions. It began in the 1970s when it became counsel to City Investing, which at that time owned GDC.

Mr. Dodyk himself began representing the parent in 1978, and he said he represented the subsidiary through the first half of the 1980s. In 1984, the same year Ms. Allen signed the contract, Mr. Dodyk defended GDC in securities litigation. Other Cravath attorneys performed the due diligence for the 1985 initial public offering, he said, when the company became independent.

His more intense involvement began in 1987. At that time, New York's Sullivan & Cromwell had managed to satisfy the Federal Trade Commission's concerns about the company's operations, but Mr. Brown testified that the firm had warned him GDC might face "criminal" problems with the banks that bought its mortgages because of the skewed appraisals.

Mr. Brown called his former colleague, Mr. Dodyk, and asked him to take a "fresh look" at what was known inside the company as the "secondary mortgage market problem." At about the same time, the civil suits began to pour in, and Mr. Dodyk's portfolio was expanded to include the company's response to them.

The former Rhodes scholar, who graduated fifth in his 1964 Harvard Law School class, said on the witness stand that he and other Cravath attorneys began a close examination of each part of the GDC sales program and found it legal. Therefore, if each element were legal, Mr. Dodyk concluded, the program itself had to be legal.

"I couldn't see how" anyone could claim otherwise, he said repeatedly throughout his testimony.

Mr. Dodyk did not reach this opinion easily. Indeed, it was reached with the thoroughness of investigation and legal analysis expected of Cravath. After the fall of 1987, as many as nine of the firm's attorneys—joined by as many as 20 attorneys from other law firms—set to work. In addition to exhaustively researching state and federal laws, Mr. Dodyk and his colleagues interviewed as many as 40 GDC employees, including Mr. Brown and the other defendants, and reviewed thousands of land contracts and appraisals, and the documentation relating to the civil suits. His team also talked to appraisers and the secondary lenders, reviewed the depositions of the plaintiffs and visited the GDC communities, he testified.

Cravath's Analysis

He interpreted the plaintiffs' allegation that the home buyers were defrauded through the assumption of mortgages higher than the value of their homes to be nothing more than a charge that GDC's prices were higher than those of local builders.

"We told General Development management that it was not a violation of law to charge a price which was higher than the price which the local builders were charging," he testified. "In an economy such as ours, a seller is free to charge whatever price he chooses."

He advised the company that the Southward Ho trips were legal because the trips had originated long before the price disparity had become a problem.

"I found no case, state or federal, which said that the activities of a GDC salesman, in keeping the customer focused on the GDC product, could be deemed an act of fraud," he said.

As for various strategies the company used to prevent its customers from discovering the market value of their home: "I told the company that a seller does not have a duty to disclose its competitor's prices. I told the company that GDC had no duty to try to predict and tell the sellers what the resale prices would be of its houses."

The program of swapping paid-off lots toward purchase of a house was fine too, Mr. Dodyk reasoned, because there was no false statement made and it could be viewed as a discount on the price of the house. The appraisals were no problem either. The peculiar method GDC used for them was disclosed to the financial institutions before they bought the mortgages. The appraisals were prepared for the banks after the purchasers bought their houses; thus, the purchasers could not have relied on them. He adopted the point of view that the fact that GDC provided financing for the home buyers also could not be part of a scheme.

"Seller financing of commercial products in this country is commonplace," Mr. Dodyk testified. "So the mere act of lending money to a purchaser seemed to me not under any of the case law to be possibly describable as a scheme to defraud."

He first reached this conclusion, Mr. Dodyk said, in November of 1987 and reaffirmed it repeatedly in his representation.

On May 8, 1988, Mr. Dodyk was asked to address the GDC board, which included such heavy hitters as former Florida Gov. Reuben O'D. Askew, then a senior director of the Miami law firm of Greenberg, Traurig, Askew, Hoffman, Lipoff, Rosen & Quentel P.A., and Howard L. Clark Jr., then executive vice president and chief financial officer of American Express Co.

He reiterated his view to the board that the complaints against the company were meritless. In a follow-up letter, he said the civil lawsuits were "solely the result of the effort by two or three lawyers in the Miami area who are instigating and financing that litigation.

"There is nothing wrong legally or morally with the practices which these lawyers are attacking," he wrote.

***

Ultimately, Mr. Dodyk's logic did not wash with the jury. Mr. Brown and another defendant were acquitted Aug. 5 of the fraud counts but found guilty of the conspiracy charge. They face five years in prison, $250,000 in fines and restitution claims in the millions. Two other GDC officers were found guilty of all counts and face sentences of 8-12 years and millions in fines and restitution.

The defendants indicate they plan to appeal the conviction, and the appeals court may at last vindicate Mr. Dodyk's reasoning. But perhaps he and the other members of GDC's legal team, for all their legal analysis, failed to supply a jury of Florida citizens with an adequate answer to the question posed by one prosecution witness.

Vasuderareddy Kethireddy is an Indian immigrant who also bought a GDC home in Port Malabar. He, like Ms. Allen, admitted on cross-examination that he had not read the contracts and other documents he had signed.

"But the point is, here the GDC is trying to protect themselves through those clauses," Mr. Kethireddy said. "The real, the cheating thing behind it, is that basically you are selling $34,000 worth of house to a person from out of town for $70,000. Now, how do you get a person to buy a $34,000 market value house for $70,000 unless you have done deceptive practices?"

Editor's Epilogue

The judge sentenced the four General Development Corp. executives to prison terms ranging from five to 10 years. In March 1995, a federal appeals court ordered them released from prison while it considered their pleas to overturn the verdicts. A civil lawsuit over Cravath's work with the GDC was still wending its way through the courts by the end of 1995.

Give 'em Hector

Michael Hudson,
Mother Jones, July/August , 1994

The man from Jim Walter Homes climbed the paint-starved wooden steps and banged on the front door. Brunilda Benavides had to kick the door open. It was sticking. As usual.

He was there for the money. He said she was three months behind on her mortgage for the one-story house that Jim Walter Homes had built for her in Premont, Texas.

She explained she'd never missed a payment on the place—not until her lawyer advised her to stop paying because the house was full of defects and dangers.

She says he snarled: "That's why you Mexicans don't have anything. Because you don't pay. Why don't you pay what you owe?"

She shot back: "Why don't you fix the house?"

Her husband Oscar, who has cerebral palsy, came to see what the yelling was about.

Benavides says the collector screamed at her husband, too, calling them both gang members. Then her husband had a seizure.

Her cousin, Robert Perez, came over and chased the collector off the property. Benavides and Perez say the Jim Walter man kept yelling from the street: "You all are Mexicans, and you're never gonna have nothin'."

***

Across the wildflower strewn flatlands of South Texas, many Mexican-American families have stories to tell about Jim Walter Homes and its powerful Wall Street owners. They tell tales of warped floors, sinking foundations, bad plumbing, and foreclosed hopes. From Premont to Corpus Christi to San Antonio to Laredo, more than 400 families accuse the $2.5 billion conglomerate of targeting them for a massive scam built on the very dream of owning a home. Those low-income and working-class Texans claim the company profited handsomely by selling them shoddy homes at inflated prices.

"Every place you go where they have Jim Walter Homes,

you're gonna find people who are pissed off," says the home-owners' attorney, Hector Gonzalez. "Because they prey on poor people's hopes and dreams."

Now, some South Texas homeowners are striking back. They are suing Jim Walter Homes and its owners, an invest-ment group led by Kohlberg, Kravis, Roberts & Co., the lever-aged buyout firm of "Barbarians at the Gate" book and movie fame. In 1988, KKR and its backers leveraged $2.4 billion to swing their "friendly" buyout of Jim Walter Homes and its sis-ter subsidiaries.

For its efforts, KKR made an initial 700 percent return on the $5 million stake it put into the buyout. "It's a pretty fair return," KKR partner Henry Kravis conceded during a 1989 hearing, not long before the business took a turn for the worse. Three months later, Jim Walter Homes filed for Chapter 11 bankruptcy protection, in what was at the time the biggest financial collapse of a company taken private in a leveraged buyout.

Gonzalez and his clients have sued KKR and Jim Walter Homes in Texas and have pursued them into federal bank-ruptcy court in Tampa, Florida. For Gonzalez, a freewheeling small-town attorney who revels in South Texas's rough-and-tumble image, it's a case in brown and white: honest, hard-working Mexican-Americans facing down some of Wall Street's most powerful dealmakers.

Jim Walter lawyers say there's no legal rationale that could possibly link KKR and Kravis to construction com-plaints in Texas. But Gonzalez has tried to do so in the law-suits—and he's tried to make it a personal matter. In Court papers, Gonzalez refers to "Henry Kravis, hereinafter called Defendant Henry." Gonzalez says over and over that Kravis has used the money that the homeowners have paid on their houses "to make donations to New York museums so he can get social prestige."

Gonzalez claims in one lawsuit that KKR and Jim Walter Homes are using bankruptcy court as a "criminal haven" to protect themselves from the homeowners' lawsuits.

All the while, Gonzalez has tried to bait Jim Walter Homes into a showdown in Texas. He's instructed his clients to stop making their monthly payments—daring the company to come into the courts in South Texas and foreclose on the houses. This stubborn, brush-country rebellion has already cost Jim Walter Homes more than $3 million.

***

Brunilda Benavides says it's time people know how Jim Walter Homes treats its customers. Five years ago, she and her husband were living in a one-bedroom trailer with three children. One day she ran into a woman putting up a Jim Walter sign.

Benavides says the saleswoman gave her the pitch and asked how much her family earned. She explained that her husband was disabled and they got by on a few hundred dollars a month in public aid. She says the woman said Jim Walter Homes could put them in a good home for $200 a month.

That was on a Friday. The next Monday, Benavides says, the company delivered lumber to a plot of land her family owns. The saleswoman told her, "Your application went through." Benavides asked, "What application?" She says she hadn't signed any papers. Still, it sounded like a good deal, and she wanted to get her family out of their cramped trailer.

From the start, though, things didn't go right. She says the painters didn't come until months after the house was finished. She says a "hot" wire was left exposed inside a kitchen outlet, the doors and windows never opened or closed properly, and the water heater quickly broke. The house is full of warps and cracks. The roof leaks. "They promised us a quality home," Benavides says. "When they promise a quality home, what do you expect? A good home, not junk."

***

Jim Walter Homes is one of the South's most recognizable homegrown corporations, a longtime Fortune 500 member that has built more than 300,000 houses across the Sun Belt and into the midwest. From company headquarters in Tampa, Florida, its corporate parent, Walter Industries, has grown from one of the nation's largest builders into a diversified giant with stakes in manufacturing, coal, and gas.

Jim Walter officials say they have a record of fair dealings with their customers. "We don't build bad houses to take advantage of poor people," company spokesman David Townsend says. "We have thousands and thousands of customers who've been in our homes for years, and they're very satisfied." As for the sheer number of Gonzalez's clients, a company lawyer says, "It's not hard to accumulate clients when they're put in a position where they don't have to make any payments for a while."

Townsend says it's inconceivable that the company's collectors would harass a customer, or that a salesperson would forge signatures to push through an application. Jim Walter himself, the man who gave the empire its name and remains its chairman, has said his company's goal is to "treat others only as we would have them treat us."

The story of Jim Walter has been told again and again. The year was 1946. Walter, a 23-year-old Navy vet and newly-wed, borrowed $400 from his dad and bought a tiny, unfinished house in Tampa. Three days later he sold it for a $300 profit. Then he talked the builder into a partnership. They built a couple of model "shell homes" that were unfinished inside. Their first Sunday of business, they sold 27 homes for $1,000 each.

Walter's shell homes looked good to war veterans and the working poor. Buyers put up their land for security and kept the price of their houses down by doing part of the inside work themselves. In return, Jim Walter offered two enticements: No down payment. Easy financing.

By 1955, Walter had set up a mortgage subsidiary and collected $1.2 million in expansion capital through a stock offering. By 1964, the company made it to the New York Stock Exchange.

Jim Walter Homes had become one of corporate America's great post-World War II success stories. But following this up-by-the-bootstraps story was another, darker tale: a 25-year history of lawsuits and government investigations.

• In 1978, Kentucky's attorney general sued over complaints that the company had built houses with serious flaws and lousy materials. Jim Walter Homes agreed to pay more than $1 million in investigative costs and refunds to about 850 of the 2,100 customers who had bought houses over six years.

• In 1979, Mississippi's attorney general investigated Jim Walter employees who allegedly used forgery and harassment to force homeowners into paying thousands of dollars above their mortgages. One collector wore a T-shirt warning, "If you don't pay, you don't stay." The company—which says it was as much a victim of the scam as the homeowners—fired some employees and settled out of court with the homeowners.

• Through the 1970s and early 1980s, the company was sued by hundreds of customers in Texas, Georgia, and other states who charged it with collection abuses, fraud, and other lawbreaking. In Elberta, Georgia, the company lost a $200,000 jury verdict and then settled out of court with an uneducated woman who claimed she had been manipulated into buying a home she didn't want. According to testimony, a salesman had sealed the deal by having her 9-year-old son sign the contract.

***

Nowhere has Jim Walter Homes had more legal problems, however, than Texas. And most of those cases can be traced to one man: Hector P. Gonzalez. Gonzalez was a high school dropout from a Brownsville barrio who joined the Air Force at 17 and went on to become a lawyer. He is a hefty, rumpled man who is as comfortable quoting French or Mexican history as he is telling tales of his legal wars across South Texas.

Gonzalez began his campaign against Jim Walter Homes in 1976, when a former client came to him with complaints about his shell house. He won $30,000 for the man, and more cases followed. It wasn't easy. He says the company smothered him with legal paperwork and high-priced lawyers. During one heated deposition, he fought back by grabbing a Jim Walter lawyer and stabbing him in the back—with a pencil. Gonzalez was called before the Texas bar for a disciplinary hearing to answer why he'd done that. "Because I didn't have a knife," Gonzalez replied. His license was suspended for 60 days.

But the fight paid off. In 1980, he won more than $4.1 million for about 350 clients to settle claims that the company was charging higher mortgage rates than Texas law allowed. Then in 1981, he and another attorney won well over $3 million for 756 clients to settle lawsuits alleging shoddy building practices.

But Jim Walter Homes thought it had found a way to get rid of Gonzalez. They say they agreed to the 1981 settlement only because Gonzalez promised never to sue again. Gonzalez says the only promise he made was not to sue for seven years.

In the next years Gonzalez was content to build his own personal injury practice Then in 1989, the daughter of an old client walked into his office. Déjà vu: a complaint about a Jim Walter house. "It was the same story," Gonzalez says. "Promises. Representations. Lies. Fraud." More than seven years had passed, and Gonzalez couldn't turn away the child of a client. Come to my office on Sunday, he told her, and pass the word I'm going to take Jim Walter cases again.

He expected three or four families, but 45 showed up. "Oh shit," he thought. "Here it starts again."

Sylvia Vela Lopez was there that day. She bought her house in Alice in 1981, when she was 23. "I was so young. I was a single parent. I said 'OK. We can afford it.'" But she says the house had problems from the start. Her closet doors were so out of kilter, for example, that she replaced them with curtains. When she fell behind on her payments, she says, collectors would "call my mother and tell her things" or yell at her in front of her neighbors. Despite her husband and father's best efforts to fix them, the floors are still warped.

Suzanne Burroughs' house in Banquete has cracks all over the ceilings and walls. It sags so much to one side there's a one-inch gap between the kitchen counter and the wall. "The thing that gets me: They would hire just anybody to do the work," says Burroughs, one of a handful of Anglos in the suits. "I'm not saying an 80-year-old man can't do it, but I felt sorry for him. It took him forever." Now, she wants the company to haul the house off her lot. "I come from a good family. And I was used to having nice things. This was supposed to be my dream house, and it's a joke."

Jim Walter officials contend that many of their legal wrangles have been blown out of proportion. Still, they concede that the Kentucky suit was "a black eye"—and that there are problems with some of the houses in South Texas. They say they would fix them if Gonzalez would drop his demands for a multimillion-dollar settlement.

After Gonzalez sued, company employees inspected 201 houses. Jim Walter lawyers said they would give homeowners "the benefit of the doubt" on many claims and come up with $330,000 for repairs—an average of $1,633 per house.

David Fowler, a University of Texas engineering professor who has worked as an expert witness for Jim Walter Homes, says that most of the problems stem from poor maintenance on houses that average more than 10 years in age. But he did find foundation problems with six or seven of the 25 he inspected after the current litigation began. "Like any builder, they're going to make some mistakes," Fowler says. "I haven't detected any kind of scam where they're trying to rip somebody off. In general, I've found Jim Walter makes a pretty good house."

David Castro disagrees. A former city inspector in Corpus Christi, Castro has checked about 600 Jim Walter Homes as Gonzalez's building expert. Not one met minimum building codes, Castro contends. He says the problem with these houses is building defects and cheap materials, not poor maintenance. Castro estimates most of the houses he's inspected in the last four years need $10,000 to $20,000 each in repairs.

Joe and Noemi Morales say they've already put thousands into fixing up their house in Alice. "But it's still getting the same way again," Joe Morales says. Tom Trinidad, who lives in Saspamco, says he's done all sorts of repairs, such as replacing a wooden joist that fell through the living room ceiling. "To me, Jim Walter is a good company," Trinidad says. "But I think they hired those guys who did the work, the carpenters, real cheap." When his daughter, Cynthia Ritzen, had a Jim Walter house built last year, she also had complaints. "I figured since this lawsuit was going on, maybe they would do a better job," Ritzen says. "And they didn't."

As more people have signed on, the legal battle has taken on the air of a social movement. The homeowners collected 7,000 signatures from friends and neighbors and sent a petition to Texas Attorney General Dan Morales asking him to investigate Jim Walter Homes. When Gonzalez wants to meet with his clients, he rents the VFW Hall in Alice. They pack the place. Taking the microphone at a recent hall meeting, Noemi Morales, a school teacher, exhorted the crowd: "We have to stand united in order to win this case. We're all together in this."

Gonzalez first sued in Texas, but the company had the case moved to the U.S. Bankruptcy Court of Judge Alexander Paskay in Tampa. Gonzalez has objected. He claims in one lawsuit that Paskay "does not bother concealing how little he thinks of Texas jury verdicts or of construction-related complaints."

Gonzalez contends in the suit that no matter where or what he and his clients sue for, the case will be moved to Florida. "With the threat of Paskay, the Defendants insulate themselves and the monies their illegal conduct obtained..."

Jim Walter officials say Gonzalez's allegations are ridiculous. David Townsend says that the company's bankruptcy was caused not by Gonzalez's lawsuits, but by asbestos claims against Celotex, a former subsidiary that Jim Walter Homes sold in 1988. The cloud of that litigation, combined with turmoil in the financial markets, left the company unable to repay $600 million in bonds. However, Paskay recently cleared Walter Industries of any liability for the Celotex claims.

Company officials are circumspect about their longtime nemesis. "I like Hector," company attorney Warren Fraizer says. "I talk to Hector. He calls me all the time. He called me yesterday. But I can't tell you why he put some of the things he did into his complaint."

Judge Paskay has been less restrained. During court hearings, he referred to Gonzalez as "Speedy Gonzalez" and "Little José." Paskay also questioned the English of two homeowners. Told they spoke fluent English and had in fact served in the Army, the judge said, "Whose army, Mexican?" The Congressional Hispanic Caucus called for Paskay's removal. A federal judicial panel ruled those remarks and others he made were "inappropriate," but said he could stay on the bench.

Gonzalez expects the court battle to drag on for a long time. In the meantime, he and the homeowners are trying to shame Jim Walters into caving into their demands. Over the years, Gonzalez has developed an odd relationship with the company—the dance of two old enemies who are bound together and know each other's secrets.

Once, Gonzalez says, Jim Walter officials even approached him: What could they do to avoid these hassles? How could they keep their customers from suing them?

"I told them, 'Just advertise your houses as pieces of shit. Then they can't say you lied to them.'"

He shakes his head and laughs. "They didn't take my advice."

Editor's Epilogue

In 1995, Jim Walter Corp. and Hector Gonzalez's clients reached an undisclosed settlement in their legal battle. Under the terms of a confidentiality agreement, Gonzalez was uncharacteristically silent about the case.

Part VI
Driven to Debt:
High-Priced Car Loans and Insurance

In America, our cars and trucks define us. And to a large degree, the way they're sold defines the American marketplace. It's a tough, competitive business, and the sales techniques are often equally brutal. Back in 1970, Roger Rapoport wrote in *The Atlantic Monthly* about his two weeks as a novice car salesman. "Get them to love that car," he was advised. "Make them cream all over it." When it came time to close the deal, a veteran car salesman told him, say, "Give me your OK!"

"Don't say signature," the veteran advised. "That scares people."

Not much has changed—at least not for car buyers who are economically vulnerable. "For people who have bad credit, you're gonna have to take what they give you," said Rick Matysiak, special investigations coordinator for the Georgia Department of Insurance. "If you want to drive today—as they say in the business." In Tampa, Florida, one of the nation's largest car dealers ran newspaper ads urging people with bad credit to call and ask for "Betty Moses"—a made-up name that hints, perhaps, of outcasts reaching the promised land. Royal Buick and a loan officer at Florida National Bank then falsified paperwork to secure loans from the lender. Many buyers quickly defaulted, losing their cars and their down payments. The banker and more than 20 Royal Buick employees were convicted of fraud. In Texas, ClayDesta National—a bank controlled by Clayton Williams, the unsuccessful Republican candidate for governor in 1990—had to repay $1.3 million to low-income, black and Hispanic customers who'd been forced to buy credit insurance with their car loans.

Last-Ditch Loans

Bankrupts Who Drive Are Lucrative Market
To a Growing Lender
Credit Acceptance Corp. Uses High Rates of Interest and Plenty of Repo Men

A Deal for Used-Car Dealers

Michael Selz,
The Wall Street Journal, **June 28, 1995**

SOUTHFIELD, Michigan—It is only midafternoon, but Credit Acceptance Corp. already has heard from more than 2,200 beleaguered borrowers.

As banks of employees take notes on computers, hundreds of customers a day explain why they can't pay this month. Many others want to know what will happen to their cars, which the company has repossessed. Still others are frantic because Credit Acceptance has garnisheed their wages.

It is a lending world J.P. Morgan would never recognize. Most of the customers already have defaulted on other debts or filed for personal bankruptcy. Most have turned to Credit Acceptance because no one else will lend them money. Yet Credit Acceptance approves almost every application it gets.

Charging interest rates of up to 30 percent a year where usury laws permit, Credit Acceptance mostly helps high-risk borrowers buy high-mileage cars. The borrowers often pay twice or more what the cars cost the dealers. Some decline to buy warranty contracts and end up owing money on broken-down vehicles they can't afford to fix.

Target Market

Lending to this underclass of consumers has become a thriving business for entrepreneurs such as Donald A. Foss, Credit Acceptance's 50-year-old founder. Since the company went public three years ago, its earnings have doubled and its stock price is up tenfold. Credit Acceptance doesn't originate loans but purchases them from used-car dealers.

Critics say lenders like Credit Acceptance foster financial irresponsibility when they show that even declaring bankruptcy won't keep someone from getting a car loan. But typical borrowers, such as Marianne Thomas, say they have little choice.

Mrs. Thomas, a German immigrant and 48-year-old mother of five, had defaulted on her debts in 1991 following a divorce. When she bought a seven-year-old Mercury Topaz in 1993 with Credit Acceptance financing, she says she thought its $2,300 price was high. The loan's interest rate of more than 20 percent also seemed steep. But, she says, "I was desperate for a car to get to my job." She earned $5 an hour as an aide at a home for the mentally retarded near her residence in Steubenville, Ohio.

The car overheated and stalled on the highway the day she bought it, Mrs. Thomas says. A friend, now her husband, repaired it. But eight months and more breakdowns later, she was behind on her payments. A spinal injury suffered in an auto accident kept her from working, she says.

Gone

One morning last July, Mrs. Thomas awoke to find the car had been repossessed. In November, Credit Acceptance sold it at auction for $525. The company claims she still owes $677, although she says it hasn't been trying to collect it.

Few enterprises go after such borrowers more zealously than Credit Acceptance. Some critics assail its aggressive collection methods. Others question the company's low level of reserves against loan defaults and the way it claims to protect itself against them—a two-step system of initially paying car dealers for only part of loans it buys from them, and then pooling these loans.

But the methods seem to work. Although intensifying competition for high-risk borrowers has prompted talk of an industry shakeout, Credit Acceptance last year earned $20.6 million on revenue of $54.5 million. Its portfolio of high-risk used-car loans has tripled over two years to $553 million, the company has a stock-market value of more than $900 million, and Mr. Foss's stake alone is worth more than $550 million.

Drive It Away

This is heady success for the son of a used-car dealer who took a job selling paint instead of going to college. In 1967, Mr. Foss opened his own used-car lot on Detroit's dealer-heavy Livernois Avenue. He sold his first car, a 1959 Sunbeam convertible, for $100 down and a promise from the customer to pay the balance at $25 a week. "I'm still waiting for the first payment," he says.

As the business grew (he now owns about a dozen dealerships), the lots began spending as much time arranging financing as making sales. In 1972, Mr. Foss formed Credit Acceptance to centralize the task. Today, the company arranges high-risk loans for more than 2,000 auto dealers in 48 states and Britain.

It serves a growing market. So far in the 1990s, over four million Americans have filed for personal bankruptcy—as many as in all of the previous 10 years.

As competition for unblemished borrowers has intensified, financial institutions are soliciting more of those they used to reject. One measure: The number of credit-card accounts that require a security deposit has more than doubled since 1992, to 915,000 last year.

More than a quarter of the people who file under Chapter 7 liquidation proceedings of the Federal Bankruptcy Code are extended credit within two years, according to a study by Purdue University's Credit Research Center. Within five years, more than half are borrowing again, often from lenders like Credit Acceptance.

The researchers suggest that lenders even may find former bankrupts ideal customers: In addition to emerging from court debt free, they are barred from filing for bankruptcy again for seven years.

But lending to this market takes its own set of skills. In terms of where it expends its efforts, Credit Acceptance is as much a collection agency as a lender. At the state court in this Detroit suburb alone, the company in 1993 and 1994 filed some 800 civil suits against Michigan customers, mostly to collect money lent.

Two-thirds of Credit Acceptance's nearly 300 employees

spend their time tracking down delinquent borrowers, persuading them to pay and arranging the seizure of their cars and wages when they don't. In customer service, for instance, Brenda Holm does nothing but handle inquiries from customers who have fallen behind.

It's stressful work. "The customer may be screaming and yelling, but I'm not going to yell back," she adds. "If they use foul language, I'll terminate the call."

Credit Acceptance says its tries to keep borrowers in their cars as long as possible. But when it loses confidence in a debtor's ability or willingness to pay, repossession often follows, as James W. Little discovered. The Cleveland resident had been in financial trouble before. In the late 1980s, he and a woman he describes as his former common-law wife defaulted on $30,000 in debt they had accumulated buying a car, furniture and household appliances, he says.

Despite his experience with overspending, Mr. Little says, he bought a six-year-old GMC Sierra in 1993 to use as a second car. He says he borrowed the $3,000 down payment against his tax-deferred savings plan at work. At the time, he was earning $13 an hour at a frozen-foods plant.

Mr. Little says he began falling behind on his payments last year, after his employer fired him for taking too many days off. He had been missing work to drive his mother to a hospital for kidney dialysis, he adds. Credit Acceptance seized his truck last September, the month after his mother died, he says. Credit Acceptance won't comment on the repossession.

Credit Acceptance says it ultimately seizes one out of 10 cars it finances. About 1,600 times a month, the company turns to a nationwide network of repossession agents, who usually charge $200 per car. Customers can get their vehicles back, though it usually costs them a payment equal to the sum of the overdue amount, repossession expenses, and two additional monthly installments on the loan.

Repo Man

Repo-department manager Wayne Mancini says he must judge his company's chances of getting all its money before returning a repossessed car to a borrower. "If we know the customer can continue to make payments, we're going to let them back into the vehicle," he says. "If we get a pretty good idea they're going to try to stiff us again, we're better off selling at auction."

He says Credit Acceptance's goal is to fetch at auction at least 30 percent of the account's unpaid principal and of the interest that would accrue if the loan were carried to full term. To recover this balance, the company is free in most states to garnishee the wages of its customers.

To Mr. Foss, such practices are business as usual. "If you advertise for people who are poor credit risks, you shouldn't be surprised when they don't pay," he says.

Some critics, however, contend that the company's methods can be irresponsible. Without telling his mother, Marcia Baker's teenage son Matthew three years ago signed a Credit Acceptance loan with a high-school friend who wanted to buy a car. Matthew, now 21, also pitched in half of her down payment. The 1984 Mercury Caprice broke down within a week. When the dealer who sold the car refused to repair it, Mrs. Baker's son and his friend had it towed by the city.

The Indianapolis mother says she learned of the matter only when Credit Acceptance called her home to warn her son that his first monthly payment was overdue. He eventually defaulted on the debt, and his friend moved away. "I feel like a fool," he says.

His mother feels worse. Allowing teenagers with no credit experience to commit to a $3,000 used-car loan is immoral, she says. "His dad and I would never have allowed him to do this. He was just trying to impress this girl," she adds. "He had no idea of the financial ramifications." Credit Acceptance says the youth never made a single payment. It adds that it lends to people with no credit as well as to people with bad credit.

A Call at Home

Others claim, in complaints to state regulators, that Credit Acceptance's methods can be abusive. Wilbur Nichols tells bitterly of the time two years ago when, he says, he and his wife received a call at 9:45 p.m. from a Credit Acceptance employee over $25 in late-payment fees that Mr. Nichols disputed.

The Kentucky resident, who filed for personal bankruptcy in 1988, had borrowed nearly $4,300 at an interest rate of 22 percent to buy a car. He says that when his wife, who answered the phone, complained about the hour of the call, the bill collector said, "Look, bitch, your name isn't even on the loan. Get off the phone and get your husband." Mr. Nichols says he then took the phone. In the argument that ensued, he says, the caller threatened, "We will get our money. If you can't pay, we'll come and get the damn car."

Mr. Nichols says his credit rating has improved enough that he refinanced the loan through a credit union. But he also complained about Credit Acceptance's practices to the state attorney general. In a letter to the attorney general. Credit Acceptance denied the couple's version of the incident and claimed Mr. Nichols was the one who began using foul language.

Other critics say Credit Acceptance's accounting practices may be as aggressive as its bill collection. The company has reserves for potential losses equal to only 1 percent of its loan portfolio. That is one-seventh the level of reserves at Mercury Finance Co., Northbrook, Illinois, the largest used-car finance company. Yet Mercury makes much more conservative loans and says only 0.8 percent of them are 60 days or more past due. At Credit Acceptance, where more than 25 percent of loans are at least 120 days overdue, the lower reserves boost reported earnings, but possibly expose the company to future write-offs.

The Pool System

Credit Acceptance says its reserves are sufficient because it obligates dealers to accept much of the risk for loan defaults. Like many other auto-finance companies, Credit Acceptance buys loans from dealers at a discount. But unlike companies such as Mercury, it initially hands over to the dealer only part of the loan's discounted purchase price, in the form of a so-called advance.

Credit Acceptance says it combines the debt it buys from each dealer into pools of 100 or more loans. It pays dealers the rest of their money only after recovering enough from borrowers to cover a pool's dealer advances. The pooled money it withholds mitigates the risk that borrowers will default before Credit Acceptance recovers all of its up-front payments, says Richard Beckman, vice chairman and chief financial officer. In such a case, Credit Acceptance doesn't have to pay the dealer the balance of the loan purchase price. And it can make up its loss on the advance out of loan repayments it otherwise would have handed over. The dealer, of course, commonly mitigates its risk by charging a higher price for the car.

During the first quarter, $12.1 million of loans, or 2.2 percent of Credit Acceptance's portfolio, went into default, according to its unaudited quarterly securities filing. But with the pooling mechanism, only $310,000 of those defaults were charged against reserves, Mr. Beckman says.

The company's loss-protection method "works better than any other model I've ever seen in high-risk lending," says Michael Corasaniti, an analyst in New York for Alex. Brown & Sons Inc.

But the practice troubles Paul R. Brown, a New York University professor who edits the *Journal of Financial Statement Analysis.* Dr. Brown, who analyzed the company at *The Wall Street Journal's* request, notes that there is little explanation of the risk pooling in Securities and Exchange Commission filings.

"Given that there is hardly any discussion of this crucial element to their protection, one has to doubt how thorough the company is in implementing it," Dr. Brown says.

Indeed, the loss-protection system relies on Credit Acceptance's exercising the discipline to withhold funds from dealers even as a growing number of competitors are advancing more money to auto lots.

Nearly a dozen companies offering high-risk auto finance have gone public in the 1990s. The heightened competition is prompting some to give dealers larger amounts up front.

Three months after signing on this year with Credit Acceptance, John Leclair, owner of Luke's Auto Sales Inc. in Springfield, Massachusetts, says he is jumping ship. "I'm done with Credit Acceptance," he says. "I've found a 10-times-better deal."

Others also foresee pressure. "Clearly there's more competition in this market," says Thomas Fitzsimmons, a Credit Acceptance director and partner at William Blair & Co., the Chicago firm that underwrote Credit Acceptance's initial public offering. "So there's probably going to be price-cutting and some type of industry consolidation."

However fierce the competition gets, Mr. Foss vows that his company will remain a market leader. In a display of ambition that belies his cherubic face and unassuming presence, he adds: "I'd like to be in the Fortune 500 some day."

Mercury Finance

Steep Incline

Andrew Bary,
Barron's, **August 15, 1994**

In the lending business, a 1 percent return on assets is considered healthy, and a 2 percent return is beyond most banker's dreams. How, then, does a smallish Illinois auto-finance company achieve a stunning 9 percent return on its $900 million of assets? In short, by lending to customers the banks shun, by charging annual interest rates that run to 40 percent, and by quickly repossessing cars from any deadbeat borrowers.

The company in question, Mercury Finance, has become a stock market darling the past few years, and now sports an astonishing market value of nearly $2 billion. That's enough to rank Mercury right up near Boston's Shawmut National Corp. or New York's Republic National Bank or California's H.F. Ahmanson, all big regional financial institutions that have more than 30 times as many loans outstanding as Mercury does.

But don't be surprised if Mercury starts to feel a few bumps on the road ahead. For starters, rising interest rates could squeeze its profit margins. Also, a host of feisty competitors, inspired by Mercury's success, are now crowding into the business of making auto loans to America's "credit-impaired." And lastly, a court verdict in Alabama last week raises questions about the way Mercury has achieved its stellar profits, particularly Mercury's practice of booking loans far larger than the amounts ever advanced to the car buyers.

These factors may make it difficult for Mercury to keep increasing its earnings at the 25 percent annual clip sought by John Brincat, the company's president and chief executive officer. Yet judging by Mercury's stock price, most investors seem to think growth will continue with nary a hiccup. At the current price of 16 1/4, Mercury shares trade at eight times book value, while traditional lenders trade at maybe twice book.

Mercury's stock price amounts to 29 times last year's earnings, and 22 times this year's expected earnings of 73 cents a share.

In an interview, Brincat says growth concerns are legitimate, but he insists Mercury has the right people and controls in place to expand its current 23-state network of 235 offices, now heavily concentrated in the Southeast. A former U.S. Marine and 25-year veteran of the finance business, Brincat runs his company with Prussian efficiency and with a keen eye on costs. He'd rather hire retired military officers as loan officers than traditional bankers, because military men "understand discipline and responsibility" and can better deal with Mercury's customers, who often have histories of late payments on their bills or bankruptcies.

This preference for officers may partly reflect Mercury's early days, when it opened offices around military bases and focused on lending to the service ranks. This proved a shrewd move because the young enlisted personnel had regular salaries, lived in a regimented environment and couldn't easily try to stiff Mercury by leaving town with their cars.

As Mercury has grown, however, the percentage of its loans that go to military men and women has shrunk to under 10 percent. The company says its growth opportunities lie in the civilian market, which holds promise but also greater risk than military-related business.

Nowadays the typical Mercury loan goes for a five-year-old car, carries a rate of 22 percent, runs 2 1/2 years. The typical borrower is a blue-collar worker with a spotty credit history who needs the car to get to work. Many people have a knee-jerk aversion to the used-car business, but Brincat says it's cleaner than ever: "There's this image of a gravel lot on the wrong side of town where you drive by in the morning and see five cars, three with their hoods up and battery chargers on and one getting its tires pumped up. We do most of our business with franchised new-car dealers. These aren't skid-row types."

Perhaps that's one reason why new lenders are getting into the business just about every week. Even giants like North Carolina-based NationsBank are starting to make loans to auto buyers with impaired credit records. Bill Fellows, sales manager with Star Chevrolet in Tallmadge, Ohio, says it's now much easier for customers with blemished credit to get financing than ever before.

One investor who harbors doubts about Mercury is Matthew Lindenbaum, a principal at Basswood partners, a Paramus, New Jersey, money manager that specializes in financial stocks. "You can't argue with Brincat's record over the past 10 years, but it's harder to grow at 25 percent a year when you're starting at a $1 billion base of loans than at $100 million," says Lindenbaum. "When finance companies expand at that kind of rate, bad things often happen."

Mercury features a solid balance sheet with more than a 20 percent equity cushion, and it did make a shrewd move last year in extending the maturity of some of its debt. Yet it still relies on short-term financing for a third of its capital base, making it vulnerable to higher rates. And as it grows, it will have to pay higher costs than it's now paying for borrowings.

Mercury's business practices hadn't resulted in any major legal troubles until last week, when an Alabama jury awarded a Mercury borrower a staggering $50 million in damages. The borrower, Willie Ed Johnson, purchased a 1985 Chrysler three years ago from a used-car dealer in Dothan, Alabama, for nearly $3,700, and got a 30-month loan at a rate of 26.3 percent. The car, meanwhile, had been purchased by the dealer for $1,900 and was available for cash for $3,000.

To finance two forms of credit insurance from Mercury, plus the car, Johnson got a loan for just over $4,000. Mercury, however, bought the loan from the dealer for just $2,700. This transaction illustrates a common industry practice of purchasing used-car loans at a significant discount from their face value. Mercury argues that the discount offers it protection against credit losses and should be of no concern to borrowers. The company compares it to the common practice whereby Visa or MasterCard pay merchants less than the face value of items paid for with credit cards. But on Johnson's loan, the discount was more than 25 percent, as opposed to the 2 percent typical on credit card purchases.

Mercury's practice of regularly purchasing loans for less than their face value helps to keep down its credit losses to under 0.5 percent annually. This buffer, which the company calls dealer reserves, totaled $68 million on June 30, and acts as a first line of defense against losses, often allowing Mercury to avoid dipping into its loan-loss reserves.

The Alabama jury ruled that Mercury effectively was a direct lender to Johnson and thus should have disclosed the amount of the discount, and the fact that the discount made the borrower's annual interest rate exceed 50 percent a year. Johnson's car was eventually repossessed, sold for $500, and he was left owing Mercury about $6,500, money he couldn't pay.

An expert witness called by Johnson's legal team was Gene Marsh, a law professor at the University of Alabama. Marsh says he had never seen a reserve arrangement as large as the one in the Johnson situation: "I'm no Ralph Nader, but to me it's a very simple idea. How can it be right to collect money that was never disbursed? Even the car dealer said this financing arrangement caused them to raise the price of the car."

Marsh adds that Alabama is a mecca for financing companies like Mercury because it has no usury limit on loans above $2,000. What's more, Mercury and others make a lucrative business of selling life, disability and involuntary unemployment insurance to borrowers in Alabama and elsewhere, policies that have drawn fire from consumer groups for their high rates.

Mercury says the jury in Barbour County, a jurisdiction notorious for huge damage awards, basically rewrote Alabama law in reaching its decision. Mercury says it scrupulously adheres to state and federal lending laws wherever it operates.

The jury's award, $90,000 in damages and $50 million in punitive damages, is unlikely to stand, given the $6,500 loss suffered by Johnson. But investors still have to worry that the verdict itself might be upheld, or that Mercury could be hurt by subsequent class-action suits filed by Johnson's lawyer.

Even if Mercury ends up paying nothing to Johnson, delivering on Brincat's ambitious growth goals may prove tougher than his fans suspect.

Editor's Epilogue

The trial judge reduced the punitive-damages verdict to $2 million. Mercury then settled out of court for a lesser amount.

Country Justice

Why a Mississippi Jury Found a Small Dispute Worth $38 Million

Trustmark Bank's Treatment of a Struggling Family Didn't Seem Neighborly

Mr. Smith's Car Troubles

Martha Brannigan,
The Wall Street Journal, **April 12, 1995**

LAUREL, Mississippi—In disputes with banks, regular folks usually don't win.

Then there is Ken Smith, a 25-year-old oil-rig worker who lives in a double-wide trailer with his wife and two children. He doesn't have much money—holding his job depends on the fortunes of the oil industry—but his family says he is doing the best he can. "He's the finest young'un you ever want to meet," says his father-in-law, J.W. Holmes.

In 1987, when Mr. Smith, just out of high school and newly married, bought a new $9,200 Nissan Sentra, his father-in-law was happy to co-sign the car loan. The loan was bought by Trustmark Bank, a unit of Trustmark Corp., a regional bank-holding company with total assets of $4.76 billion. But the way the bank treated this family turned out to be one of the most costly things it ever did.

There were thin times for Mr. Smith and his wife, Clancy, a 24-year-old receptionist, and often they were late with the car payment. Trustmark played hardball. One September morning, when Mrs. Smith went to take their six-year-old daughter to school, the car was gone—her handbag and the girl's schoolbooks still inside. Only after calling the sheriff to report it stolen did she learn the bank had sent a tow truck to repossess it.

With help from Clancy's parents and a local lawyer, the Smiths got their car back. "All the bank had to do was call me, and I would have paid it," says Clancy's mom, Joann, a part-time seller of Mary Kay cosmetics. Whenever she learned her daughter and son-in-law were having trouble with car payments, she marched to the bank herself and dropped off a check.

When Mr. Smith was unemployed, which happened from time to time, he let his car insurance lapse, too. But, like most banks, Trustmark's rules say you must have insurance. So, when he couldn't make the payments, the bank bought its own insurance for the car—at three times the price of the Smiths' policy.

Surprise in the Mail

After five years, the Smiths finally paid off their car, and they thought they were finished dealing with Trustmark. But, they got a surprise in the mail: a bill from the bank for an additional $9,500 to pay for the costly coverage Trustmark bought when the car was uninsured.

The couple were shocked. They didn't have that kind of money. And they felt they never authorized the bank to buy such expensive insurance in the first place. They went back to their attorney, Alfred Lee Felder, a family friend. Mr. Felder then teamed up with Lawrence Abernathy, a local lawyer who keeps a pot of pink-eyed peas simmering on the stove in his store-front office.

The hometown attorneys, familiar with the way local folks think, said people here would surely understand the frustration of fighting with a bank and side with the Smiths. Foisting that hefty insurance bill on the young couple, the lawyers said, was "a story about corporate greed."

Trustmark said it did nothing wrong. The bankers were so sure they were right, they wouldn't even talk about settling.

But they picked the wrong people—and the wrong place—to fight. Laurel is a lumber and oil town of 22,000, and its people are used to hard work and hard times. They are sympathetic to struggling families, suspicious of big institutions.

Bossed Around

"One of the things that characterizes the Mississippi mind is an enduring sense of grieving that somebody, sometime, somewhere did us wrong, a serious injustice," says David Sansing, professor emeritus of history at the University of Mississippi in Oxford. "The feeling is big companies live off the sweat of our brow."

And feisty juries are nothing new in these parts. In 1859, a Mississippi jury ordered a railroad to pay $4,500 to a passenger because a train blew by his stop by three-quarters of a mile and refused to back up, according to a *Mississippi Law Journal* article by Jackson attorney John G. Corlew. He writes that cotton companies, utilities and insurance firms have all played the role of the bad guy with deep pockets.

Still, Messrs. Smith and Holmes weren't thrilled about having to go to Jones County Circuit Court. "I had to miss a whole week of work to get this over with," Mr. Smith recalls. "I about wore my one sports coat out."

Jurors took a liking to Mr. Holmes, 56, a plain-spoken oil-rig supervisor fond of fishing, hunting and Cajun cooking. He is active in the local Baptist church, recently using his tractor to clear a field for a new cemetery. He explained that the bank never even told him about the expensive insurance. In fact, the bank wouldn't even tell him the name of the company that sold it. Trustmark said it wasn't obligated to notify him—even though he co-signed the loan, and even though the squabble resulted in a black mark on his otherwise fine credit. After the spat with the bank, he was turned down for a Texaco credit card, his first-ever rejection.

'Smoking Gun'

Trustmark said it sent out three notices about the insurance to the Smiths, though the couple deny ever receiving them. The bank said the whole thing was the family's tough luck. "If these people don't like the price of the insurance— and it's high—they can go get their own," Trustmark's attorney, William Goodman, said recently.

A big break came in the case one morning when Mr. Abernathy, the family's attorney, found that someone had slipped a plain white envelope—the "smoking gun," as he calls it—under his door. Inside was a copy of an internal bank memo, dated March 1991, from Robert Gaddis, president of Trustmark's Laurel branch. In it, he warned management that the "collateral protection insurance" premiums it was charging were "extremely high, almost to the point of being ridiculous."

"We are going to find ourselves in the middle of a class-action suit that could turn out to be very expensive," wrote Mr. Gaddis, outlining a list of concerns. He added: "We have had one threat from a lawyer here in Laurel, and if his brain hadn't been pickled by alcohol, he would have probably picked upon this coverage and filed ... suit." But Trustmark bosses never paid attention to his suggestion, Mr. Gaddis later testified in court.

Perhaps they should have. Other companies have found that sticking people with high-priced insurance payments isn't such a great idea. In 1993, Ford Motor Credit Co. paid $58.3 million to settle class-action claims that it had overcharged customers for collateral protection insurance in California. That same year, Barnett Banks, Inc. agreed to pay $19 million to Florida customers in a similar class-action suit. In February, NationsBank Corp., based in Charlotte, N.C., agreed to settle a class-action claim in federal court in Miami for $6.2 million.

Humbling Experience

Jurors here in Laurel thought Trustmark was gouging the Smiths. And they also didn't like the fact that the bank was getting fees from the insurance company. The bank said the fees were for handling paperwork. The family's lawyers called the fees "kickbacks," a depiction that rang truer to the jurors.

As the local lawyers predicted, most of the jurors felt they understood the trouble average people have dealing with banks and insurance companies. "If it had happened to my husband and I, we'd have been up there, too," says Eunice Morris, a homemaker on the jury.

So, in January, the panel ordered the insurer, Jackson-based Ross & Yerger, and Trustmark to pay Mr. Holmes a total of $500,000 as compensation for his troubles. They didn't give Mr. Smith any money, but they gave him clear title to his car. Then Judge Billy Joe Landrum told the two men and 10 women of the jury to come back the next day to consider punitive damages.

The next morning, the lawyer for the insurer told jurors just what they wanted to hear: insurance executives were "humbled" by the jury's reprimand, and went back to their motel that night to think about how they could change their ways. The insurance company was stuck with $375,000 of the award, which was equal to 25 percent of its net worth, he said. He implored the jurors not to pile on more damages. They didn't.

Trustmark, however, was firm and unrepentant. Jerry Watkins, a millwright who served as the jury foreman, says that even after the verdict was read, Trustmark officials "were still up there saying, 'We've done nothing wrong.'"

The jury thought the bank had a bad attitude. In hopes of teaching Trustmark to be more sympathetic to its customers, they ordered the company to pay $38 million—$19 million to Mr. Smith, and $19 million to his father-in-law.

In deciding the amount, the jury picked up on an idea: They chose $38 million because it represented 10 percent of Trustmark's net worth. One juror had suggested fining the bank 20 percent of its net worth, while somebody else suggested 1 percent. So they considered 10 percent to be a fair compromise, and a fitting punishment.

"It seemed like a conspiracy between the bank and the insurance company to really stick it to people who get in a financial bind," Mr. Watkins says. "We wanted to send a message to the insurance companies and financial institutions to straighten their act up."

The award is one of the largest in cases where no one was hurt and no property was destroyed. The decision is "shocking," says Mr. Goodman, the lawyer overseeing Trustmark's appeal, "not only because of the amount, but because of the underlying facts. This is not somebody who had both arms cut off by some negligent person."

In his corner office, with burnished wood furnishing and thick Oriental rugs, Mr. Goodman is confident the award will be reduced or set aside. "It's got to be," he says. "You can't just have a system where people go off in a room and put zeros down. What if it was $138 million, or $238 million?"

Next week, a hearing is set to determine whether the

award is to be cut or overturned. Mrs. Holmes says she would like to give 10 percent of anything she receives to her church. But, so far, the family hasn't seen any cash.

Though the jury made them both instant millionaires, Messrs. Smith and Holmes returned to their oil rigs immediately after the trial. "This isn't the lottery," Mr. Holmes says.

Editor's Epilogue

The trial judge cut the total award to $5.5 million. Trustmark is appealing the jury verdict. A federal judge has certified a class-action suit involving an estimated 20,000 borrowers who were charged for forced-placed insurance by Trustmark.

Part VII
No Place Like Home:
The Business of Slumlords

In his 1974 book, *Mortgage on America*, Leonard Downie, Jr. documented how slum landlords buy up buildings, take out mortgages based on inflated property values, cut maintenance and then reap huge tax writeoffs for depreciation—doing all this with the generous help of mainstream financial institutions. Republic Savings and Loan in Washington, D.C., for example, went from $10 million in assets in 1957 to $57 million in 1967—thanks mainly to mortgages made to slumlords. Decades later, slumlords and speculators continue to get rich without much hindrance from government or the news media. And tenants keep on suffering. Rats were so common at Doris Ruffin's apartment at 142 West 140th Street in Harlem that she gave one a name. She stopped paying her rent the day "Herman" jumped onto her bed. The building's front door had no lock, there was no heat or hot water, and the elevator wouldn't budge. The landlord ignored the decay, even after a judge's order to make repairs. Then one day the building's east wing collapsed. Three of Ruffin's fellow tenants died.

Making Millions Out of Misery

The money flows from hand to hand, and a building falls in Harlem.

Kim Nauer, Andrew White and Jesse Drucker,
City Limits, **May 1995**

To gain a solid grasp of professional real estate investors' motives and methods, listen to how they refer to the buildings they trade. They call the properties "sticks and bricks." And when neophytes confuse a building's concrete foundations and sturdy floors with a solid financial investment, the pros call this a "sticks and bricks fixation."

That's because they have something more important on their minds: cash, profit margins, return on investment. "It's the cash flow that's coveted. Real estate is a mere means," writes Gaylon Greer, author of a popular textbook published by Dow Jones & Company.

In New York City, acknowledged to be one of the nation's most cutthroat real estate markets, a thriving industry has been built on the successive waves of newcomers who fail to make accurate, realistic calculations about cash flow before buying property. They allow themselves to be convinced that, one way or another, the buildings they buy will be their ticket to wealth.

Two months ago, the east wing of a large apartment building at 142 West 140th Street in Harlem collapsed, killing three tenants and revealing in very stark terms how low-income people pay for the errors of ill-educated speculators. Marcus Lehmann and Morris Wolfson, the principals behind Mount Wilson Realty, the company that owns the felled building and at least 11 others, owe millions of dollars in debt on their overleveraged properties and are likely to lose their buildings to foreclosure. They may also face criminal charges stemming from the March 21 tragedy.

Much less evident, however, are the investors who make profits—often big profits—from the business of slumlording. Alternately known as financiers, mortgagees or operators, this group makes loans that banks with strict credit rules are unwilling or unable to make. They play the role of negotiator and matchmaker, hooking up buyers, sellers and people willing to invest capital for the high interest returns that risky inner-city investments have sometimes garnered.

A *City Limits* investigation of the Harlem properties bought and sold by Mount Wilson over the last decade shows that nearly all were originally purchased with capital from the private, unregulated world of alternative financing. Lehmann and Wolfson's financiers loaned them money—lots of money, at very high interest rates—during the mid-to-late 1980s, while the city's real estate market was hot and the values of buildings in low-income neighborhoods were soaring. Impressively, but in what appears to be standard fashion, these operators got out of the deal and took their profits with them just moments before Mount Wilson began to show signs of serious financial trouble.

All of this happened in a market boosted by what experts say were wildly inflated property values made possible by crafty financiers, reckless—often foolish—speculators, and bankers who drove their own institutions into the ground, only to be bailed out by America's taxpayers as part of the Savings & Loan crisis. As a result, the federal Resolution Trust Corporation (RTC) ended up with hundreds of millions of dollars worth of mortgages on inner-city properties—including all of Mount Wilson's Harlem buildings.

Yet the financiers behind Lehmann and Wolfson made money, and today they are still among the biggest players in the business, plowing cash earned in New York's marginal neighborhoods during the 1980s into investments in shopping malls, parking lots and other properties around the country. And the mortgages on Mount Wilson's buildings have been sold by the federal government to a new set of financiers at rock-bottom prices. According to business press reports, these new investors expect that their multimillion-dollar investment will yield a whopping 100 percent profit.

Jethro Chappelle, a 69-year-old resident at 75 St. Nicholas Place, which is, for the time being, still owned by Mount Wilson, knows that he and the other residents will never see a penny of this windfall. Living on the fifth floor with a wheel-chair-bound son, Chappelle and other family members have been lobbying for months to get the building's elevator fixed. Chappelle adds that he and his family have been calling building management for the last two years about a three-foot hole in his bathroom ceiling. Rats, which crawl on the rafters above, sometimes fall through onto the floor below. Now Chappelle, like most tenants interviewed for this article, just wishes he could move. "I'm sick and tired of the whole damn thing," he says.

A survey of property data on five blocks surrounding the West 140th Street building shows that during the last 10 years, only a small minority of the private property mortgage deals in the neighborhood have involved traditional bank financing. It's a problem that afflicts most low-income communities of color, where high-interest alternative financing is often the only game in town.

Unlike banks, which negotiate a mortgage to last several decades, private financiers set up short-term deals, commonly called balloon mortgages, with high up-front interest payments and early principal due dates. When the principal comes due, the financiers have the flexibility and the option to renegotiate the deal. If, for example, the cost of money has gone up, they can charge higher interest rates. If the deal has begun to look shaky, they can find other investors to buy out the mortgage loan.

On the surface, it appears that the financiers are taking a high-risk gamble that the landlords they lend to will be able to keep up with their mortgage payments. But real estate watchers say the true professionals, the ones that last in this business, know how to control their risk and get out of the market before the inevitable downturns.

Mount Wilson's deals follow this pattern. Property records show that Lehmann's and Wolfson's early forays into the real estate business were largely privately financed, with high-priced loans from two closely linked backstage players well known to tenant activists in the South Bronx and Harlem.

In the case of 142 West 140th Street, Mount Wilson bought the six-story, 71-unit building for $525,000 from a Yonkers businessman in January 1987. The partners put down $100,000 in cash and signed a $425,000 mortgage note at 15.5 percent interest with Howard Parnes, a partner in the Scarsdale-based company, Houlihan-Parnes Realtors. At the end of the year, Parnes attempted to sell the mortgage to Marine Midland Bank. The bank apparently balked and quickly returned the mortgage to the financiers.

Parnes then sold the mortgage to Harvey Wolinetz, another operator whose office shares the same Scarsdale address. And Wolinetz turned around and promptly loaned the building owners—Lehmann and Wolfson, a.k.a. Mount Wilson—another $175,000.

By this time, Lehmann and Wolfson had to make mortgage payments of $93,000 a year to Wolinetz on this property alone. Meanwhile, they had purchased a dozen more buildings in the surrounding neighborhood, mounting up debt at a rapid pace.

They had owned the building barely a year when Wolinetz, having collected tens of thousands of dollars in payments and, in all likelihood, broker's fees as well, cashed out. Wolinetz sold the mortgages, and the risk, to Ensign Savings Bank. And Lehmann and Wolfson promptly borrowed another $450,000 from Ensign against the value of the building.

Because none of the players in the deal returned calls from *City Limits*, there is no way to know exactly what happened to the money. A Bronx real estate operator familiar with the process says the best analysis is simple: don't get obsessed with the sticks and bricks, just follow the cash. Lehmann and Wolfson put $100,000 down on the original purchase, and after the Ensign deal they had $450,000 cash in hand. Whether or not they reinvested any of that cash back into the building through repair work is unclear. Lugarna Thompson, who lived in the West 140th Street building for 54 years, say residents have had only minimal services for the last five years.

What is known is that, within a few months of signing the deal with Ensign Bank, Lehmann and Wolfson, under the new name "Mount Wilson Stores," bought another building on Flatbush Avenue near Park Slope, Brooklyn, for $675,000. They may have been investing their Harlem earnings in another part of town.

There are variations in the histories of Mount Wilson's many Harlem properties. In some transactions, for example, buildings were repeatedly flipped between Parnes affiliates and a Brooklyn-based real estate company. But for each of the Harlem buildings examined by *City Limits*, the epilogue was the same: After a period of intense trading during the height of the speculators' market, the mortgages were sold to Ensign Bank. In February 1990, the bank cemented its relationship with Lehmann and Wolfson with a massive $10.5 million mortgage loan that wrapped together 13 buildings worth a total of just $6.3 million, according to an RTC appraisal one year later. The bank also loaned another $1.7 million to the pair.

Two months later, Mount Wilson stopped making their mortgage payments to Ensign. And in September, the bank, heavily invested in the city's collapsing real estate market, was seized by federal regulators.

In 1990 and 1991, Lehmann and Wolfson were hit with nearly two dozen lawsuits and liens, ranging from unpaid oil bills to personal injury claims. Their corporation, Mount Wilson, filed for bankruptcy protection in the fall of 1991, owing RTC principal, interest and fees on $12.7 million in Ensign loans, according to court documents. The city was also seeking more than $800,000 in back taxes and other charges on their properties.

As Lehmann and Wolfson's finances spun out of control, the lives of their tenants steadily worsened. Interviews with some 20 tenants, activists and lawyers involved with the buildings indicate that the owners all but refused to do work there. While tenants' fortunes differed depending on how well organized they were, all reported that maintenance in the early 1990s was done almost exclusively through the Department of Housing Preservation and Development's Emergency Repair Program.

With Lehmann and Wolfson protected by Chapter 11 bankruptcy proceedings, Mount Wilson's mortgages were put up for RTC auction. They were quickly purchased, along with Ensign's other bad debts, by an investment group led by

Lloyd Goldman, nephew of deceased New York real estate king Sol Goldman, and investment banker Michael Sonnenfeldt. According to *Crain's New York Business*, the $45 million deal is expected to net them more than 100 percent profit. Interestingly, Houlihan-Parnes bid $55 million for the same failed loan package; the RTC, however, rejected Parnes' higher offer, charging a conflict of interest. RTC officials, however, would not elaborate.

Today, Mount Wilson's buildings remain in limbo, riddled with code violations, heat problems and desperately needed repairs. In addition to the liability associated with the collapse on West 140th Street, Mount Wilson owes the city $911,000 in back taxes, water and sewer charges and emergency repair bills for the building and its other Harlem properties. The company has also been cited for more than 5,000 housing code violations, nearly 1,000 considered hazardous.

Tenants report that they have been fighting for repairs for years, frequently hiring lawyers to bring Lehmann and Wolfson into Housing Court. The companies in charge of building management shifted repeatedly over the years, finally resting in 1992 with Baruch Singer of Triangle Management. In four Mount Wilson buildings on West 108th Street, tenants report that Singer is making repairs, but they say he is also following up with an aggressive eviction policy and, occasionally, steep rent increases. Other buildings deeper in Harlem crave even this attention. "They always say, 'We're working on it,'" says Jacqueline Goodman, a tenant in 406 West 129th Street, which, aside from the collapsed building, could qualify as Mount Wilson's worst. Goodman says there's been a hole in her son's bedroom for more than a year; the gash in her living room ceiling went so long without repairs that HPD was forced to fix it. This is the only maintenance she can get, she says. "Any work that I have done here is done by Housing."

Singer wouldn't be interviewed at length for this article. He did, however, indicate that Mount Wilson's tenants should get used to him. Contrary to press reports, he says he has only taken charge of the properties in order to purchase them. "I have always been negotiating to buy these buildings," he says.

As shrouded as the world of private financing may seem, it's an industry as old, and as legitimate, as the free market system. And mining bank-snubbed neighborhoods has long been considered a prime opportunity for up-and-coming operators.

"Redlined regions—the areas from which large lenders will not entertain loan applications—are not necessarily poor prospects for lenders; they just require you to weigh more carefully the merits of each individual parcel that a borrower wants to pledge," writes Gaylon Greer in his text for real estate pros. "Since you will expect to make loans repeatedly in the same geographic area, you can afford to spend some time and money mastering the economic eccentricities. The payoff goes on and on."

In Harlem and the South Bronx, Howard Parnes and a coterie of closely-linked associates are well-known to tenant activists and housing lawyers. They report that he has long had a reputation for allowing buildings to deteriorate under his watch.

In the late 1970s and early 1980s, he was a prime player in the game of "flipping," buying a building at its legitimate cost and quickly reselling it to a burgeoning market of new immigrants, uneducated on New York City's housing prices and strict rental laws. Frequently, activists says, the new owners couldn't keep up with the steep mortgage payments and Parnes would foreclose, taking the building back to sell to another unsuspecting buyer. At the height of the real estate speculation market in 1986, *The New York Times* reported that Parnes had a hand in financing an estimated two-thirds of the residential property transactions in the Bronx.

Today, Houlihan-Parnes remains a high-profile broker of properties throughout New York City and, indeed, nationwide. Parnes' company has also branched out to take advantage of one of the 1990s' most lucrative real estate opportunities: the default mortgage market. Reports in *Liquidation Alert*, an industry publication, show the firm to be a substantial investor in the mortgage clean-up business.

These players should not be ignored by tenants and organizers seeking services from a negligent landlord. They will often respond to some well-timed in-your-face pressure, says Mary Dailey, executive director of the Northwest Bronx Community and Clergy Coalition, which has been combating—and carefully researching—the predations of the speculative mortgage market for more than a decade.

Oftentimes, she says, mortgagees like Howard Parnes will give a landlord some breathing room on his or her payments in order to ensure that major repairs are made—if the tenants are applying enough pressure in the right place, or if lenders feel it's necessary to head off city enforcement action and other legal headaches, she says.

Two years ago, the tenants at 2275 Morris Avenue, a 25-unit Bronx walkup, were having no luck getting their landlord to deal with mounting code violations and drug dealers who had taken over apartments in the building. When they stepped up pressure by filing a case in Housing Court and seeking intervention from the state's Division of Housing and Community Renewal, they also made sure Parnes and Barry Shapiro, the building's two mortgagees, received copies of every official document. For good measure, the tenants even stopped by Shapiro's Bronx office for a long, unscheduled chat.

"We perked up his ears," Dailey laughs. "Next thing you know, the landlord is talking to us, saying, 'You know, sending Howard Parnes everything is not doing you any good.'"

"I don't know if Parnes ever gave this guy any time off on his mortgage or not," she adds. "But they got the repairs done in the building."

Advocates caution, however, that these are not permanent fixes. If over-mortgaging is the problem, the only way to get a building back into good economic and physical health is to reduce the debt burden. To do that, the landlords must have access to government-backed, low-cost rehabilitation funding and, more importantly, legitimate long-term financing. Or the tenants themselves might swing a deal to buy the property on the foreclosure market, a technique that the Community and Clergy Coalition has used to create tenant cooperatives and community-owned housing.

For now, however, the tenants in Mount Wilson's buildings can only continue to pressure for repair work—and hope that Baruch Singer, if he does buy the buildings, is able to borrow money for the mortgage and maintenance without beginning the cycle anew. "It makes you feel very uneasy," says Emma Moore, a tenant on West 108th Street. "We don't want what happened on 140th Street to happen here. We don't want to wake up and find ourselves in the basement."

Life on the Edge

The powerless often are forced into apartments that defy city housing codes and, in some cases, belief

Jim Morris,
Houston Chronicle, **March 26, 1995**

Irving Carrillo's grandmother was drawing a bath for him the moment he scampered out the unlocked door of her third-floor bedroom, went through the balcony railing and landed on his head 30 feet below.

Then a scrawny 2-year-old, Irving took his plunge at the Princessa Apartments the afternoon of Feb. 14, 1992, about a month after he and his mother had moved into the decaying Spring Branch complex. His grandmother, with whom they were living, had complained to management for some time about the broken lock on her bedroom door, but it hadn't been fixed and she was using a small board to secure it.

Irving, consequently, had no trouble getting out. And once he was on the balcony he had no trouble passing through old metal balusters that were nine inches apart, more than twice as wide as city code would allow for a new complex.

Irving fell to the sidewalk and crushed the front left part of his skull. By the time his mother, Berta Carrillo, arrived at the complex from work, the boy had been loaded onto a stretcher and was barely conscious.

"I was scared to death," she said. "His eyes were swollen shut. Blood was coming out of his mouth."

Irving spent the next eight days in the intensive-care unit at Ben Taub Hospital. Initially, it appeared that he would die. "The priest was at the hospital the first day and the second day," his mother said.

Now 5, Irving miraculously survived his fall with no permanent physical impairment or disfigurement. But brain damage greatly diminished his cognitive skills, and he faces years of learning and language difficulties—especially heavy burdens for a shy, Spanish-speaking child of immigrant parents.

His parents and thousands like them who come to Houston legally and illegally from Mexico, El Salvador, Vietnam and other Third World nations face harsh working conditions, slum apartments and an array of other hardships. Fearful of authority and confused by the American system of government, they are unlikely to complain about hazardous conditions or discrimination. They are easy prey.

"Immigrants are people, too. You almost have to say that nowadays," said Nestor Rodriguez, a professor of sociology at the University of Houston who has studied the migration and settlement patterns of Central Americans for 10 years. "We're a society supposedly concerned about quality of life, be it in education, health or housing. Not to care about those things degrades our standards."

Because immigrants often make less than minimum wage, Rodriguez said, they are limited to the cheapest housing.

"They feel they're lucky to get a place, especially during the initial stages of settlement," he said. "I've found immigrants from Central America sleeping under trees and behind dumpsters. We're seeing a lot of disadvantaged people, very vulnerable but having few resources to acquire better housing."

At the time of his near-fatal accident, Irving Carrillo was living in a 22-year-old complex owned by Abraham Weiss, a former jeweler from Brooklyn who got into Houston's low-end apartment market in 1988.

Out-of-state investors like Weiss, as well as some local ones, are attracted to older apartment complexes in certain Houston neighborhoods for several reasons.

The buildings are relatively inexpensive to buy and—depending on management philosophy—to maintain.

Houston's 115 neighborhood-protection inspectors can't track down every dangerous apartment among the city's 2,500 complexes; by necessity they respond mainly to complaints.

Perhaps most important, Houston has a huge immigrant population—an estimated 100,000 people from Central America alone—with a constant, urgent need for cheap housing in areas of heavy commerce. They are reluctant to move once they have settled, even if the carpet is filthy or the balcony railing is pulling out.

They seek out places that don't require big deposits and background checks. They get, in return, apartments that may lack hot water in the winter or air conditioning in the summer.

They may be plagued by roaches and rats. They risk death, injury or displacement by fire. Although the fire marshal's office is supposed to perform an annual inspection of every commercial building in Houston, Chief Ernest Brinkmann said his 48 inspectors reach only about 20 percent of the apartments in a given year. In 1994, 1,584 apartment fires in the city killed seven people, hurt 49 and did $11.5 million in damage.

The totals since 1988: 41 dead, 333 injured, $70 million in damage.

Bea Link, Houston's assistant public works director for neighborhood protection, tires of hearing landlords defend themselves by saying they provide a public service: low-cost housing for poor people who probably don't speak English and probably aren't in the United States legally.

Link has seen, among other things, children with gaping sores on their legs from contact with raw sewage. "No one should have to live in conditions like that," she said, "even if they're paying $10 a month."

Until recently, Houston showed little inclination to punish apartment owners who let their properties deteriorate. Lagging behind cities such as Dallas and San Antonio, it had no independent code-enforcement body until the Building and Standards Commission was created in April 1992 and no blanket ordinance to deal with crime-ridden or structurally unsound buildings until December 1993.

"Houston has a different mentality," said Dallas attorney Maxine Aaronson, director of Texas Neighborhoods Together, a statewide alliance of 650 neighborhood and civic associations. "It's the same reason they don't have zoning: It's your property, and you should be able to do what you want with it. That, unfortunately, exploits a lot of people."

A Chronicle reporter and several photographers recently toured eight complexes in five areas with large immigrant populations: Gulfton, Spring Branch, Greenspoint, Park Place and northeast Harris County. The visitors saw broken windows, exposed wiring, wobbly stairways, collapsed carports, mounds of garbage and many other hazards, and spoke with angry tenants who pay upwards of $400 a month for apartments that flood repeatedly because of bad plumbing.

Children are everywhere in these complexes, steering their bicycles around broken glass and playing on old balconies not designed to keep small bodies safe.

Tenants of such places typically pay market rates for substandard apartments, Link said. Their landlords "aren't doing them any favors," she said. "For most of [the owners], we find, it's just an investment. They don't put any money into maintenance. A lot of times we have difficulty getting in contact with them because they have P.O. boxes or holding companies."

Abraham Weiss' Rina Corp. owns two complexes in Houston and three in Pasadena. Weiss, who has been in real estate for 35 years, said in a telephone interview that he has spent "a lot of money" on the 324-unit Princessa since he bought it as a nearly vacant foreclosure property from the Federal Deposit Insurance Corp. in January 1988. "It was really in pieces," he said.

His son, Moe, who manages the family's complexes in New Jersey and Delaware, said the Princessa is "200, 300 percent better" than when his father took it over, although "it's not where he wants it to be." He said his father is a "hands-on" owner who "specializes in buying distressed properties and slowly but surely working them up. These [FDIC] properties were a blight on the landscape, something the governments should have been ashamed of."

The Princessa attracted the attention of the fire marshal's office after an arson fire on Sept. 14, 1990, killed a woman and her young daughter, and an accidental fire on April 20, 1993, killed two children.

Investigations uncovered a number of code violations, including the absence of smoke detectors and fire extinguishers.

And in a 1993 deposition taken in conjunction with a negligence lawsuit filed by Irving Carrillo's parents, Weiss did not sound like a hands-on owner. Asked to characterize his role in the daily management of the Princessa and another run-down Houston complex, the Villa del Rey, Weiss said, "Worrying about money, because I am losing money here."

Speculators pursue properties such as the Princessa "because they can purchase them for next to nothing, maybe dress them up with some minor cosmetics and in some cases receive federal subsidies for rent," said Houston attorney John Millard, who represented the Carrillos in their suit, settled for an undisclosed sum in May. "This is a class of tenant that's easy to take advantage of. They don't complain."

Security at most of the complexes examined by the *Chronicle* appears to be feeble or nonexistent. At the only place the visitors encountered uniformed guards and controlled-access gates—the Stone Brook Apartments on Airline Drive near Greenspoint Mall—they also saw many boarded-up units and abundant graffiti.

The Stone Brook's owner, Alfred J. Antonini of Hayward, Calif., declined to be interviewed. As of December, according to an apartment ownership guide published by O'Connor & Associates of Houston, Antonini owned or managed 15 apartment complexes in Harris County.

His properties have drawn repeated tenant and neighbor complaints about raw sewage, standing water, structural deficiencies, rats and trash, according to records provided by the city's Neighborhood Protection Division. In 1992, Antonini's Northwest Corners Apartments in Spring Branch was demolished as a dangerous building under an agreed order with the city.

Antonini also has been named in 32 delinquent-tax lawsuits filed by Harris County, the city of Houston, the Houston and Spring Branch school districts and the city of Bellaire since 1986. Lawsuits filed in 1994 alone allege that he owes $159,070 in back taxes; on March 1 he signed an agreed judgment requiring him to pay another $77,622 to four taxing jurisdictions. Michael Deeds, managing partner of Heard, Goggan, Blair & Williams, the law firm that collects delinquent taxes for the Houston Independent School District, said Antonini regularly waits until the last minute—right before foreclosure proceedings commence—to pay what he owes.

Antonini is not the only Californian whose Houston apartment complexes have drawn complaints.

On the day the *Chronicle* visited the Fairmount Apartments on Hillcroft in the Gulfton area, the main breezeway gate was open, and people walked into the front courtyard unchallenged, despite a rash of violent crimes on the property in recent years. Nine days after the visit, the owner of the complex, Terry J. Clark of Rohnert Park, Calif., paid $150,000 to settle a negligence suit by a Honduran woman who was sexually assaulted and badly beaten in the presence of her two-month-old child in her apartment the morning of May 10, 1993.

Criminologist George Kirkham, professor emeritus at Florida State University, prepared a security analysis of the Fairmount at the request of Houston attorney Tommy Gillaspie, who represented the assault victim.

In a report last December, Kirkham said his review of police records showed that the Fairmount "had long been characterized by extremely serious 'opportunistic crime' problems, including repeated violent attacks on its tenants. This notwithstanding, there is no indication that management ever sought to either become aware of the existence of such events or implement appropriate security measures to deal with them. The case record reveals that no security survey was conducted by Mr. Clark or any organization at his behest at the time he took over the complex [in 1991], despite its location in an obviously high-crime area."

In a telephone interview, Clark declined to discuss the 1993 rape. He described the Fairmount, however, as a "very calm complex" and said crime statistics that suggest otherwise are misleading. "We're being maligned a bit over there when we don't deserve it," he said.

Clark said he got into the Houston market because "prices are a lot cheaper down there than they are up here [in northern California]. I looked at a number of properties in Houston, and I like the people [at the Fairmount]. They seemed like a nice bunch of people."

Kirkham reported that Clark "repeatedly failed to react to the well-documented problem of undesirables entering the property with impunity for such purposes as loitering, drinking and victimizing tenants." A year ago Clark hired Houston security consultant Tommy Campos, who recommended that Clark install floodlights, replace a perimeter fence and make other improvements at the Fairmount; Clark has acted on many of the recommendations, Campos said.

William Brill of Annapolis, Maryland, a nationally recognized expert in apartment and mall security, has concluded that crime in apartment complexes "really isn't as random as people think it is." In most cases, he said, an assault or a burglary is the result of a decision-making process by the perpetrator as to whether poor lighting, unlimited access and general shabbiness suggest a high probability of success.

Brill is convinced that premises-liability lawsuits like the ones filed by the Fairmount rape victim and the Carrillos force apartment owners to improve security and make repairs. Houston attorney Hartley Hampton, whose firm has handled about 50 of these cases, said they are "the only tool I can think of" for low-income apartment tenants hurt in preventable accidents or preyed upon by opportunistic criminals.

"Because of the huge underclass we have in Houston, the supply-and-demand forces just aren't going to cause [owners] to try to compete with one another to provide cleaner, safer, better-run apartments," Hampton said.

Tort-reform legislation under consideration in Austin would, among other things, shield apartment owners from punitive damages in virtually all crime-related cases.

Larry York, an Austin attorney who advises Houston-based Texans for Lawsuit Reform, agreed that some landlords might concern themselves less with security if their potential liability is reduced.

"Obviously, all this is a balancing act," York said. "You may have an apartment complex that's run perfectly well, and some nut case you have no control over wanders onto the property and assaults somebody." Under current state law, he said, even the most diligent owner can be hit with punitive damages in such a situation.

Bruce Bryant, who owns two complexes in Harris County and three elsewhere in Texas, said a property need not become blighted merely because most of the tenants are poor immigrants.

Bryant said he has spent about $400,000 on his Rockwood Landing complex in Greenspoint since he bought it in 1992. He has tightened security and offers activities—swimming lessons, field trips, "movie nights"—for his 800 tenants, two-thirds of whom are Hispanic and half of whom are children. The rents he charges—$399 a month for a two-bedroom- one-bathroom unit; $420 for two bedrooms and two baths—are the same or marginally higher than those charged at complexes with less attentive management.

"I just don't want to own anything that I'm ashamed of," Bryant said. "It drives me nuts that some of these [owners] don't want to put any money into their properties. They go in and buy the place with little or nothing down, and then they don't pay their taxes or their water bills. They basically have no screening [of tenants] whatsoever. If you have the cash, they let you in."

Two state representatives from Houston, Scott Hochberg and Kevin Bailey, are sponsoring legislation that would allow court-appointed receivers to manage and order repairs on crime-ridden apartment complexes for up to a year.

"The community is victimized by these places because they look terrible," said Bailey, who was aghast when he toured Stone Brook in his north Houston district a year ago. "But the people who live there are being victimized as well, and sometimes we forget about that."

Irving Carrillo, his little sister Leslie and his parents—Hector, a Guatemalan, and Berta, a Mexican, both of whom are legal residents of the United States—have moved out of Abraham Weiss' Princessa Apartments. Weiss has replaced the unsafe balcony railings—not, he insists, because of the Carrillos' lawsuit—and spruced up the exteriors of the buildings.

But the Princessa is not yet a showplace. One of Hector Carrillo's friends offered a glimpse of his two-bedroom unit with the understanding that his name would not be used.

Mismatched sheets of linoleum covered the living room floor. The man and his wife explained that the carpet had been so dirty and smelly and they had grown so sick of complaining about it to management that they had torn it out and replaced it at their own expense.

The man ran down the list of other problems he had encountered in his three years at the Princessa, which charges him $330 a month. "The locks on the front door are bad," he said. "Water leaks in all over."

He pointed to a hole in his bathroom wall that, he said sardonically, "lets us hear what's going on in the bathroom next door." He hoped, he said, to find a new place shortly.

City Councilwoman Helen Huey, who represents Spring Branch and has led the campaign against poorly maintained apartments, conceded that Houston is "behind the curve" when it comes to cleaning up places like the Princessa.

"But we're gaining ground rapidly," Huey said. "We now have a full toolbox of very effective ordinances." From mid-1992 through 1994, the Building and Standards Commission issued 96 orders against owners of dangerous apartment complexes and assessed 27 penalties totaling $188,950.

The Comprehensive Urban Rehabilitation and Building Minimum Standards, or CURB, ordinance, the commission's main weapon, is under attack from property-rights advocates, among them landlord Alfred Antonini.

"You are trying to inflict your standards, and you blame it on landlords who don't improve [their property]," Antonini told Huey and other city officials at a public hearing on the CURB ordinance Feb. 10. "There are a lot of buildings in this city that cannot be improved."

Huey noted, however, that it is Antonini and his counterparts who have the most to lose from rigid code enforcement. "These are folks," she said, "who enjoy an economic advantage by not taking care of their property."

Part VIII
Just a Few Bucks a Week:
The Rent-to-Own Industry

Not long ago a Rent-A-Center "rent-to-own" store in Indianapolis was offering a "previously rented" Pioneer CD player for about $7 a week. It might sound like a good deal — until you check and find out that the total cost over 87 weeks adds up to $608 ... and that you could buy the same compact disc player brand-new at a retail store for $180.

For people without the cash or the squeaky-clean credit history to buy it at Sears, renting to own offers an alluring alternative: Get it today with easy payments, no credit check. But it's a costly proposition. Rent-to-own customers routinely pay three, four, five times what they'd spend on the same item at a retailer.

The industry has been tagged with many lawsuits and much criticism from advocates for the poor—but it has fought hard to counter these hits. Industry leader Thorn Americas reacted swiftly to Alix Freedman's *Wall Street Journal* exposé of its Rent-A-Center chain. It hired former U.S. Senator Warren Rudman to investigate the *Journal's* findings. His report concluded "the conduct described in *The Wall Street Journal* neither comports with Company policies nor reflects Rent-A-Center's customary business practices." It said a customer survey found 96 percent believed they were treated with respect and only 6 percent felt pressured to get merchandise they didn't want. However, another survey conducted as part of Rudman's probe found that half of employees had "seen customers who have been rented merchandise when it was apparent that they would not be able to pay for it"—and that 55 percent of employees would not recommend that their friends and family shop at Rent-A-Center.

"Rent-to-Own"
The Slick Cousin of Paying on Time

Michael Hudson,
The APF Reporter, **Alicia Patterson Foundation, 1993**

Some people call Larry Sutton "the Reverend of Rent-To-Own." Sutton preaches the blessings of the rent-to-own business with the enthusiasm of a true believer.

He owns a growing number of Champion Rent-to-own stores in Florida and Georgia: more than 20 so far. They offer televisions, stereos, furniture, washers, you name it, at weekly or monthly rates. If they pay long enough, customers can someday own these things. If they can't, the store picks the merchandise up and rents it to someone else.

Sutton likes to think of renting-to-own as something like a marriage, with the same mutual debts and duties. The hardest part of the relationship, Sutton once told a seminar of rental dealers, is getting money from customers who are squeezing by from one paycheck or welfare grant to the next. "I had one guy tell me the best close he ever used was: 'If you don't pay, the shit don't stay.'"

Sutton frowns on that approach. Rent-to-own stores have a duty to take care of their customers. "More than anything else," he said, "they are paying us to manage their money."

Advocates for the poor don't see rent-to-own quite so benevolently. They say the industry's phenomenal growth in the past decade has come by exploiting low-income people who have few choices and little political clout. According to the industry's own figures, only about one-fourth of its customers achieve their goal of ownership.

Rent-to-own customers routinely pay two, three, and four times what merchandise would cost if they could afford to pay cash. For example: A Rent-A-Center store in Roanoke, Virginia, recently offered a 20-inch Zenith TV for $14.99 a week for 74 weeks—or $1,109.26. Across town at Sears, the same TV was on sale for $329.99. Putting aside $15 a week, it would take just 22 weeks to save enough to buy it retail.

Iris Green has lived for 20 years in public housing in Paterson, New Jersey. She has no car and has never shopped outside Paterson. She paid Continental Rentals nearly $4,000 toward the purchase of a stereo, a freezer, a washer and other furnishings that had a cash price of less than $2,800. Then she got sick and the paychecks from her job as a nursing home aide stopped coming. She fell behind, and Continental came and took everything. Now she's suing the company.

"My opinion, I thought they was my friends," Green said. "I felt betrayed. I felt disgusted. I felt lonely." She told her sons to stop bringing their girlfriends over. "They had nowhere to sit."

Continental Rentals and other rent-to-own dealers say they offer fair prices and exceptional service to consumers who otherwise couldn't afford to own quality appliances or furniture.

From a business standpoint, the rent-to-own industry has been a success story of the past decade, growing from about 2,000 stores nationwide in 1982 to about 7,000 now. Estimated revenues climbed from $2 billion in 1988 to $3.6 billion in 1991.

"How can we do that by ripping off our customers?" asks Bill Keese, who directs the industry's national trade association. The rapid growth proves the industry treats its customers fairly, he said.

The industry's rise is a story of demographics and salesmanship—and lawsuits and lobbying. Legal Aid lawyers who represent the poor have fought to rein in rent-to-own, but the industry has succeeded in getting laws passed in 30 states that protect it from most legal attacks.

Rent-to-own has prospered in the marketplace by targeting the bottom third of the economic ladder. "Most of our customers are the throwbacks from the retailers that will not deal with them," Continental Rentals owner Michael Schecter said in a court deposition. "...They have limited incomes and they simply can't save money."

The industry got its start during the 1960s. State and federal governments were passing laws to control ghetto merchants who used retail installment contracts to fleece poor people. The rent-to-own industry was born during this time "as a result of the tightening of consumer credit and burgeoning federal consumer protection legislation," its trade group, the Association of Progressive Rental Organizations, says.

Rent-to-own and retail credit are essentially the same transaction: selling merchandise on time. But rent-to-own dealers have generally managed to escape state and federal credit laws because of one difference: Rent-to-own customers can bring their merchandise back any time with no obligation for the rest of the payments.

The added cost of buying on time from a traditional retailer—the difference between the cash price and the total installment price—is a finance charge regulated by state usury laws. In New Jersey, for example, retailers can charge no more than 30 percent interest each year.

Rent-to-own dealers say they are exempt from usury laws because they do not charge interest. They say the extra price of buying on time from them is a service charge covering their higher costs of doing business, such as making free repairs.

Avoiding retail credit limits has allowed rental dealers to charge much higher prices than retailers. Rent-to-own customers often pay markups that are equal to interest rates of 100 to 200 percent a year. A survey by the New Jersey Public Advocate, a state agency, turned up a store that was selling a microwave with a markup equal to 440 percent interest.

Such price advantages helped rent-to-own grow steadily in the 1970s and then boom during the uninhibited capitalism of the 1980s, when the industry produced many millionaires and prompted corporate buyouts. In 1987, Thorn EMI PLC, a British conglomerate that owned half the United Kingdom's rental market, purchased the Wichita-based Rent-A-Center chain for $594 million. The American company now has more than 1,200 stores nationwide. It claims, along with its parent, to be the largest buyer of consumer electronics in the world.

Industry officials say the bulk of their customers are working-class families and, increasingly, soldiers and professionals who move from town to town and want only short-term rentals. "The term rent-to-own, in a nutshell, is a marketing concept more than a description of the business,"

Champion's Sutton said in an interview.

Still, among themselves at least, rent-to-own dealers concede that many of their customers usually struggle to get by.

Sutton told dealers at one how-to seminar that rent-to-own stores should try to work with slow-paying customers—but you can't run a business by letting them get too far behind. You've got to get four payments every month, he advised the dealers.

"We can be good friendly Joes and we can work with 'em til heck freezes over," Sutton said. "But I tell you what, if we're getting three-for-four, sooner or later you'll be out of business. Trust me."

Getting four-for-four takes nurturing, just like a good marriage, he said. You've got to make repairs when the customer asks and keep all your other promises.

"You've got to somehow convince him that you're different than all the rest," Sutton said. "Because John's Finance Company called him about money. Fred from the car company called him about money. Jackson Brown from the clothing store called him about money. You don't want money. You've just got to get an agreement renewed."

Debra Dillard has a great relationship with the manager at the Prime Time Rentals near her home in Trenton, New Jersey. She's even become his son's godmother. Dillard, who runs a day-care business in her home, could shop elsewhere. But she prefers Prime Time's friendliness and convenience. "I pick up the phone. If I have a problem, they're there. It's solved, whether it's a repair or replacement, or I forget how to program my VCR."

She likes the idea of not getting stuck in contracts she can't escape. Also, she doesn't have to lay things away or come up with a big down payment. "That makes it easier for you to have the things you want in life."

Other customers have fewer choices. Dee Burnett is raising five children and grandchildren on welfare and food stamps in Roanoke, Virginia. For more than a year, she has been paying $220 a month to Magic Rentals for a freezer, refrigerator, stove and bunk beds. Burnett knows she's paying more than she would retail, but her divorce left her broke and ruined her credit. Once she pays Magic off, she says, she'll never go back. "From now on, if there's something I want, I don't need it right away. I'll lay it away and pay when I can."

In New Jersey, the Consumers League Education Fund has produced an anti-rent-to-own rap song that's getting some radio airplay as a public-service announcement: *With rent-to-own, your money's blown/You keep on Paying til you turn to stone.*

Critics say high prices are only part of the problem. Legal Aid lawyers charge that some unscrupulous dealers sell used goods as new, break into people's homes to repossess merchandise, charge exorbitant insurance and late fees, and use the threat of criminal charges to intimidate late-paying customers. A West Virginia rent-to-own company recently settled lawsuits by four customers who had been jailed on theft charges that were filed by the dealer but later thrown out of court.

Still, the industry has beaten back most lawsuits—either by winning favorable court rulings or by silencing unhappy customers with confidential cash settlements. This March, in Minnesota, the industry defeated its toughest legal challenge to date: a class-action lawsuit filed by Legal Aid and private attorneys charging Rent-A-Center with usury and racketeering against more than 10,000 customers. A legal team from Shook, Hardy & Bacon—a Kansas City firm known for its invincibility as a defender of tobacco companies—convinced a federal jury that rent-to-own transactions are not covered under Minnesota's retail credit act. The jury took just 90 minutes to return with a verdict for Rent-A-Center.

At the same time they've been winning in court, rent-to-own dealers have sideswiped their opponents with an effective legislative strategy: pushing through industry-written laws that provide some state regulation but allow dealers to avoid retail credit limits.

These laws require dealers to reveal basic information such as the total cost of an item and whether it is used. But critics say such laws allow rental dealers to continue charging outrageous prices. "Disclose and anything goes," some Legal Aid attorneys call it.

The industry's trade association has pushed its agenda

with well-financed lobbying.

In North Carolina, state Rep. Jeanne Fenner proposed a law in 1983 that would have treated rent-to-own deals like retail sales. The bill eventually was gutted, but the industry took revenge when Fenner came up for reelection two years later. Rent-to-own dealers as far away as Texas gave more than $6,000 to her Republican challenger—accounting for half of his campaign donations. Fenner, who spent $2,000, lost the election. When she ran for the state senate the next year, the industry gave her opponent $15,000. Fenner lost again.

Since then, attempts to regulate rent-to-own prices in North Carolina have failed.

Thirty states have passed laws that require price disclosures but give the industry safe harbor from retail credit regulations. In five of those states, consumer activists managed to win some limits on the total markup that rent-to-own dealers can charge. In Connecticut, for example, the limit is twice the cash price.

The industry has lost outright in only one state. Pennsylvania passed a law in 1989 that defines rent-to-own deals as retail sales and sets an interest limit of 18 percent a year. Pennsylvania's rent-to-own dealers claimed the new law would put them out of business, but many found a way to skirt it. They offer straight rentals—with the promise of a rebate that the customer can use to purchase the item at the end of the contract.

Nationally, rental dealers are pushing Congress to pass a national version of the industry-written state laws. Their trade association also is planning a public relations campaign that pushes rent-to-own as "an alternative way to get a piece of the American Dream."

Many dealers are diversifying their product lines, offering jewelry and even automobiles. Sutton's Champion stores have been heading upscale, offering personal computers, fax machines and beepers.

All that's fine for business, Sutton says, but you won't make money if all you're doing is peddling merchandise to a faceless public.

In August, at a seminar in New Orleans for fellow dealers, Sutton told a story about one of his store managers in Florida, a country boy with little education.

One day, a customer tried to turn in his portable TV and VCR. He had decided to get something from the Rent-A-Center down the street. The manager—who'd gone out of his way in the past to help the customer—blew up.

He ordered the customer to take his TV and VCR home—and pay his back payments right away.

"Now, two more things," the manager said. "One: Don't never, ever let me catch you taking that TV and VCR out of your room again. No. 2: Don't ever let me hear about you going into Rent-A-Center store again. You got it?"

The customer meekly apologized for momentarily straying.

Sutton wouldn't recommend teaching store managers to jump up and down like jealous boyfriends. But he said his manager did teach him an important lesson about dealing with people: "He doesn't rent televisions. He doesn't rent washers.... He doesn't sell anything. He develops *relationships* with people." The manager, Sutton noted, was his top money maker.

Peddling Dreams

A Market Giant Uses Its Sales Prowess
To Profit on Poverty

Thorn EMI's Rental Centers Push Sofas, Rings, VCRs To the
Poor at High Rates

Repos and 'Couch Payments'

Alix M. Freedman
The Wall Street Journal, **September 22, 1993**

Recording stars Tina Turner, Frank Sinatra and the
Beatles have made Thorn EMI PLC famous in entertainment
circles. But a very different group of people is now making
Thorn rich.

Though it doesn't advertise the fact, Thorn's most profitable subsidiary has nothing to do with the superstars who
record under its various music labels. Instead, the largest single contributor to Thorn's operating profit is its most obscure,
and by far its least genteel, unit: Rent-A-Center, a chain that
thrives by renting refrigerators, furniture, diamond pinkie
rings and assorted other merchandise to America's urban and
rural poor.

Since buying Rent-A-Center in 1987, London-based
Thorn has expanded it briskly, using both acquisitions and
aggressive marketing tactics introduced by the unit's top executive, a former Pizza Hut marketing whiz. Thorn now thor-
oughly dominates the industry, which is known as rent-to-
own because renters who make every weekly payment, usually for 78 weeks, become owners. Rent-A-Center USA controls
25 percent of the $2.3 billion U.S. market; the chain has more
outlets than its four biggest competitors combined.

High-Pressure Sales

Along the way, though, its high-pressure methods have
sometimes turned coercive and abusive, according to accounts
by about 50 former store employees and company executives
who have left within the past 18 months. Scrambling to meet

ambitious sales targets set under Thorn, Rent-A-Center employees routinely encourage unsophisticated customers to rent more goods than they can afford, these people say. Then, when customers fall behind in payments, Rent-A-Center repossesses the goods and re-rents them.

Customers who manage to make every installment may end up paying several times the item's retail value—at an effective annual interest rate, if the transaction is viewed as a credit sale, that can top 200 percent. In the Utah market, for example, Rent-A-Center customers pay a total of $1,003.56 over 18 months for a new Sanyo VCR with a suggested retail price of $289.98—for an effective annual interest rate of a breathtaking 231 percent.

While the rent-to-own business has always been gritty, Thorn has made it even tougher, many of those interviewed believe. Employees handling repossessions have been known to bring along members of a feared motorcycle gang as well as to vandalize customers' homes, extract sexual favors from strapped customers and even, in one instance, force a late payer to do involuntary labor.

Says Brian Baker, a former store manager in Cambridge, Maryland, "This is one of those jobs where if you have any kind of conscience you won't sleep well at night."

Now, a federal crackdown may be in the offing. House Banking Committee Chairman Henry Gonzalez, a Democrat from Texas, is expected next week to introduce a bill that would classify rent-to-own transactions as credit sales. Since some 30 states cap credit-sale interest rates at 21 percent or less, the bill would slash what Rent-A-Center and its rivals can charge. In addition, two class-action suits filed in Minnesota federal courts allege that Rent-A-Center charges usurious interest rates; one suit is pending and Rent-A-Center won the first round of the second suit, which has been appealed.

Rent-A-Center denies that its transactions are credit sales, because most customers don't end up buying the product and they can cancel at any time. Thus, it argues, it doesn't charge interest at all.

Rent-A-Center officials do concede that abuses occur and that the rent-to-own business has, in the past, been sleazier than most. But they say the company sees itself as part of the solution rather than as part of the problem. Rent-A-Center Chief Executive Walter E. "Bud" Gates points to his efforts to improve employee training, to spiff up stores and to enforce a "Respect All Customers" program that is trumpeted on wall posters in outlets. He says he is cracking down on dicey collection and repossession practices.

"The carnival industry was a down-and-dirty, nasty industry and along came Disney who rewrote the standard, and over time the whole industry came up," he says. "We're trying to do the same thing."

But former store manager Randy Richards, like many others interviewed, contends that the cleanup is in name only. "On paper, this company purified itself by introducing the new 'respect' concept," he says. But in reality, "nothing changed." He says that in 1991—a full four years after Thorn took over—he himself picked an apartment lock with a credit card in order to retrieve a late payer's living-room furniture.

A number of the former employees interviewed were fired, some for allegedly serious wrongdoing. But their accounts of working conditions and customer treatment at Rent-A-Center were remarkably uniform. Their accounts were also consistent with those of employees who quit and those of customers, even though the people interviewed came from many different parts of the country.

The $5,000 VCR

For low-income customers, Rent-A-Center has tremendous appeal. The chain gives them immediate use of brand-name merchandise, and the weekly payments are usually less than $20. But while in theory customers can eventually own the goods outright, the company says three out of every four are unable to meet all their payments.

Their failure is partially responsible for Thorn's success. The company earns considerably more by renting, repossessing and then re-renting the same goods than it does if the first customer makes all the payments. Derrick Myers, who was fired as manager of the Rent-A-Center store in Victorville, California, recalls one particular Philco VCR, for example, that he says retailed for about $119—but that brought in more than

$5,000 in a five-year period.

That means the most profitable customers are people like Minneapolis welfare mother Angela Adams, who says Rent-A-Center salespeople cajoled her into renting more than a dozen items at a monthly cost that reached about $325. Though the salespeople knew how little she earned, "they pushed it on me," she says. When she fell behind in her payments in late 1991, Rent-A-Center sued her and repossessed the goods, ranging from a bedroom set to two VCRs. Ms. Adams is now a named plaintiff in one of the two class-action suits, this one pending in federal court in Minneapolis. Rent-A-Center declines comment.

"Even if a customer can't afford it and you know it and they know it, we'll rent to them anyway," says Rod Comeaux, a former store manager from Onley, Virginia, who was fired a year ago for unrelated reasons. "We can always get it back" and re-rent it to others, he says.

Rent-A-Center's Mr. Gates denies that salespeople put excessive pressure on customers or intentionally overload them with goods. On average, customers rent 2.85 items a month, at a total monthly cost of $99.07, and they are able to cancel rentals at any time without a penalty, he points out. Store managers—who are required to obtain income and other financial information from customers—ideally should act as "financial planners" for customers, he says, adding that the "worst thing" employees can do is to rent to customers whose "eyes are bigger than their stomachs."

Rent-A-Center says its customer base is 25 percent to 30 percent black and 10 percent to 15 percent Hispanic, and just 15 percent are on welfare or government subsidies. But former store managers consistently maintain that the total on government assistance is more than 25 percent, with some claiming up to 70 percent. Indeed, they unanimously report that sales always spiked on "Mother's Day," as they call the day when welfare mothers get their checks.

How did Thorn come to enter such a harsh business? A predecessor company, Thorn Electronics, planted the seeds when it opened a rental store outside London in 1931 and then expanded the chain throughout Europe. Half a century later,

after the 1979 merger that created Thorn EMI, the conglomerate was struggling with poor results from its hodgepodge of
disparate businesses, and decided to try its luck in the rental
market in the U.S.

To get a foot in the door, Sir Colin Southgate, Thorn's
chief executive, contacted Goldman, Sachs & Co., in 1987. As
it happened, Tom Devlin, the biggest player in the fragmented
U.S. rent-to-own market, was looking for a buyer for Rent-A-
Center, the 495-store chain he founded in 1973, and he too had
approached Goldman Sachs. A deal was struck almost
overnight, with Sir Colin paying a lavish $594 million, or 42
times earnings.

Mr. Devlin stepped aside and Mr. Gates—already at
Rent-A-Center—became its new chief executive. He quickly
began buying up small competitors. Rentals now account for
almost a third of Thorn EMI's total revenue, while music—
including Thorn's EMI, Chrysalis and Capitol labels—
accounts for just a hair more.

A former senior vice president of marketing at Pizza Hut,
Mr. Gates had migrated to Rent-A-Center in 1986, after failing
to land the top job at the pizza chain. Despite his rookie status
in rent-to-own, Mr. Gates had a marketing man's feel for
demographics, psychographics, and New Age notions of customer empowerment. Inspired by some company research
indicating that his renters craved good treatment even more
than low prices, he began to merchandise respect.

Defying industry wisdom that poor customers would be
intimidated by snazzy stores, for example, Mr. Gates has spent
$40 million to make each Rent-A-Center outlet seem an ideal-
ized version of home and hearth. "Happy family" lifestyle
posters (in a store's choice of black, Hispanic or Caucasian)
adorn the outlets' walls. Prop kits dispatched from the home
office in Wichita, Kansas, provide cozy touches like plants and
print bedspreads.

Employees under Mr. Gates are required to greet customers, preferably by name, within 10 seconds of their
entrance and to conduct payment disputes out of earshot of
other renters. Stores are also encouraged to keep fresh coffee
brewing. "The customer should feel like this is home, a place

where I feel comfortable and that cares about me," he explains.

The Hard Sell

Those soft touches are coupled with hard-core salesmanship. According to a thick training manual, salespeople are supposed to quote the weekly and monthly rental rates. The manual doesn't instruct employees to quote the total cost, and former store managers say they made sure they never did. In fact, in 40 states, the total isn't even on the price tag. (Ten states require that it be listed on price tags, a rule Rent-A-Center says it will honor in all 50 states by next month.) Instead, the manual instructs employees to focus on "features and benefits," such as Rent-A-Center's free delivery and repair, and most of all, the low weekly price.

But the advertised weekly price is designed to yield each store about 3 1/2 times its cost of purchasing the merchandise from Rent-A-Center headquarters. The total is jacked up further by a one-time processing fee (typically $7.50) and late fees (typically $5). The total price is usually revealed only in the rental agreement that customers sign at the end of the sales process, former store managers say.

To boost Rent-A-Center's profits, employees also push a "customer protection" plan that offers minimal benefits but that 95 percent of customers end up subscribing to. "It's better than insurance," saleswoman Laura Daupino of the Bloomfield, New Jersey, store was overhead telling an unemployed welfare mother recently. Yet unlike insurance, it doesn't replace stolen or destroyed items, or reimburse customers for their loss. It offers customers basically one benefit: It prevents Rent-A-Center from suing customers if goods are stolen or destroyed.

For Rent-A-Center, however, the benefit is considerably larger: The protection plan is a $29 million annual revenue booster, much of which drops to the bottom line, as does most of the $27 million racked up from the other fees, according to internal company financial documents.

Rent-A-Center has long justified its high prices by citing customer defaults and the costs associated with its free repairs. But part of Rent-A-Center's secret of success is that those costs are minimal. Internal documents show its service expenses ran 3.3 percent of rental revenue in fiscal 1993, though Rent-A-Center says the actual figure is closer to 10 percent. And its total inventory losses—from junked merchandise and "skips and stolens" (as in customers who skip town)—run a bit over 2 percent of revenue.

Indeed, says Granville Quinton, Rent-A-Center's former director of budgets, forecasts and financial systems, "they have no higher skip or stolen rate than a conventional retailer." Rent-A-Center concedes that this is "technically true," but says the low rate is "misleading" because each lost item means the far greater loss of future rental income.

In part to beef up sales further, Rent-A-Center urges customers to pay their rental fees in person each week. That gives employees a chance, according to the training manual, to pitch added products. Employees are also supposed to try to "upsell," or trade up, renters to more expensive versions of the same product.

In some markets, employees are expected to hang fliers on hundreds of housing-project doors each week, in a drill known as blanket brochuring. "You would brochure the projects one week before the [welfare] checks came out so you already had that seed planted in their mind," recalls Gerald Defiore, who was fired as the store manager in Spartanburg, South Carolina. "Then the day the checks came out, you'd go back and knock on doors and fill out the work forms there. Corporate was in on it, the stores were in on it. These people didn't stand a chance." (Rent-A-Center says that blanket brochuring is optional and that targeting a project would be "logical" if it was in a store's territory.)

Complementing those tactics are an array of less savory techniques not sanctioned from above. Mr. Defiore says he scanned the obituary page, for instance, and sent cheap flower arrangements signed "from your friends at Rent-A-Center" to the bereaved. "At a funeral, everybody looks at who the flowers are from," he explains, "and when they drop by the store to thank you, you can hook them."

Rent-A-Center's Wichita headquarters staff backs up those efforts with an $18.5 million direct-mail program so sophisticated that it can tailor brochures to a single block.

Much of the blitz focuses on new prospects, primarily in six references that customers must list on an application form. (Former employees say they typically called only two references, using the rest simply for marketing purposes.) A sample letter opens like this: "Wouldn't you rather watch a big screen TV than the one you have now?"

Other targets include former customers who had failed to make all their payments: even those who have had goods forcibly repossessed receive coupons blaring in bold type, "We Want You Back." Additional letters and coupons are aimed at customers who are on the verge of paying off a product they have been renting. Some get plastic gold cards, which look like credit cards and encourage additional rentals with perks like $1 to $2 off weekly rental charges.

If Rent-A-Center salespeople are unusually aggressive, they have good reason: Their jobs depend on it. Mr. Gates has honed a tough sales-quota system known internally simply as "the plan," which calls for every store to meet weekly and monthly targets that rivals say are far more ambitious than their own. The stores' results are monitored daily by zone managers, in charge of roughly 10 stores each.

As with many other companies that use sales targets, if Rent-A-Center managers and employees exceed their quotas, they are eligible for cars, promotions and bonuses. But at Rent-A-Center, if they fail to "make plan," they are fired with extraordinary speed. In Utah's six-outlet market of 28 employees, for example, more than a dozen people were fired, including seven store managers, during the 18 months ended in July, according to two of the former managers. They say falling short of plan was the major reason, though Rent-A-Center says there were numerous factors and that some departures were voluntary.

"Rent-A-Center's employee philosophy is burn and turn," contends former Las Vegas store manager Mr. Richards, who says he quit in May 1992 because his zone manager insisted he work 80 to 100 hours a week, something the zone manager denies. "It's bring them in and work them until they can't take it any more and send them on their way," Mr. Richards says.

Mr. Gates acknowledges that the company's "total turnover should be less than half" its current annual level of 56 percent companywide (excluding headquarters) and 25 percent at the store-manager level. The company is now working to retain its people by beefing up its training programs and by evaluating employees based on customer service and other factors rather than simply on numbers, he says.

In any case, Rent-A-Center's sales and marketing strategies have produced a huge payoff. For the fiscal year ended March 31, 1993, the 1,200-store unit racked up operating profit of about $90 million on revenue of $560.3 million—a 16 percent margin that is eye-popping by retail standards. For the first time, Rent-A-Center was also Thorn's single most profitable subsidiary, contributing 14 percent of Thorn EMI's operating profit. Where store-level profit margins average 15 percent to 20 percent when smaller operators run such stores, Thorn's outlets show profit margins of 20 percent to 30 percent. Conventional retailers' store profit margins run at about 2.5 percent, according to Management Horizons Inc.

No wonder Sir Colin recently told a Las Vegas meeting of store managers that their unit was "the closest company to my heart in Thorn EMI" and that "most businessmen would give an arm, a leg and probably half their body for its performance."

Thorn executives say there is nothing insidious about Rent-A-Center's strategy of courting customers who are of limited means, and of treating them well. Customers receive "fantastic" service, says Sir Colin, who professes to be "always puzzled" why the rent-to-own industry is "badly regarded." Rent-A-Center, he adds, "treats them like kings and queens."

Customers like Carol Baker, a waitress at a resort hotel in Bolton Landing, New York, are appreciative. "The prices could be cheaper," says Ms. Baker, whose home is almost completely furnished by Rent-A-Center, "but they treat me like I'm a somebody."

Former employees and other customers see things differently. "The Rent-A-Center philosophy," says Mr. Comeaux, the former store manager in Virginia, "is that if you treat the customer like they're royalty, you can bleed them through the nose."

Repo Man

In the end, it isn't unusual for flattered customers to sign up for three or more rental agreements at a time. And some rent far more. For instance, Robert Ball, an unemployed Hunt-Wesson factory worker in Toledo, Ohio, says he is currently handing over all of his unemployment checks to pay for 13 different agreements totaling almost $900 a month.

Inevitably, some customers take on more than they can handle. So it is that behind every Rent-A-Center salesman lurks his doppelgänger: Repo man.

Repossessions are never pretty, and the pre-Thorn era was no exception. But because of the ambitious targets, people who have worked under both regimes say, employees now push harder than ever. Customers typically make their payments every Saturday and, throughout the morning, store employees work the phones exacting promises from the tardy. In these conversations, former customers say, they have been harassed, intimidated and even threatened with violence. Robert Keeling, a former manager in Gadsden, Alabama, who was fired in March in part for carrying a gun, says that a favorite ploy is falsely informing customers or their relatives that a warrant for arrest has been issued for the theft of rental property.

The telephonic onslaught resumes on Monday mornings, when 30 percent of customers are generally past due. If employees haven't reached a customer by Tuesday, they hit the road. Although it is against company rules, they often make a "milk run"—picking up payments from customers personally. Or they leave a message on the door, instructing the customer to contact them. This process is repeated all week long. If they still don't get results, it's repo time.

In the company's vans, employees comb neighborhoods looking for slightly past-due customers and the more elusive "skips." In theory, Rent-A-Center employees hew to the Fair Debt Collection Practices Act, a federal law that doesn't apply to Rent-A-Center (it covers only third-party debt collectors), but that Rent-A-Center says it voluntarily complies with. Under these rules, debt collectors can't harass customers, for example, or engage in violent or criminal acts.

Mr. Gates cites such measures as proof that he is doing his utmost to make Rent-A-Center's collection operation squeaky-clean. The CEO says his quest to transform Rent-A-Center's "profit-driven, entrepreneurial culture into a service-driven, entrepreneurial culture" is "the hardest thing I have ever done. ... I haven't gotten everyone drinking the Kool-Aid yet."

But former employees contend that Mr. Gates's strict enforcement of payment collection has in some cases actually stymied reform. Before Thorn, Rent-A-Center focused solely on the number of accounts past due, not the amount of "delinquent dollars"—or uncollected revenue. Early on, Mr. Gates decreed that only 5.7 percent (and currently 5.5 percent) of a store's total monthly rental payments can go uncollected—and zone managers have tended to set even more ambitious goals. In contrast, smaller rent-to-own businesses generally leave 8 percent to 10 percent of bills uncollected each month.

Failure to control delinquent debts "will be your downfall, so you do as much as your conscience permits," says Gary Schiefer, a former store manager in Columbus, Ohio, who was abruptly fired in May 1992 when his delinquent dollars topped 9 percent. (His former zone manager says he was fired for other reasons.) Mr. Baker, the former store manager in Maryland, characterizes repossessions as "the dirtiest part of the whole business."

It is unquestionably the most creative. On Halloween night in 1991, three Rent-A-Center employees in Utica, New York, dressed up, respectively, as the Cookie Monster, a gorilla and an alien life form and knocked on a customer's door. Once inside, they successfully repossessed a home-entertainment system on which payments hadn't been made in almost three months. Gary Gerhardt, the store manager who blessed this plan, calls the ruse "a last-ditch effort," adding, "it was the only way we could think to get someone in the door."

At the crack of dawn one Sunday, Mr. Myers, the store manager in Victorville, California, until March 1992, pulled off a particularly tough repossession by enlisting three burley Hell's Angels. He adds that in other instances he vented his spleen on delinquent customers who wouldn't come to the door by slathering Superglue all over their deadbolts and doorknobs. (Messrs. Gerhardt and Myers both were fired, but over unrelated matters.)

The grueling routine grates on some Rent-A-Center employees. Mr. Baker, the former Maryland store manager, quit in disgust in 1991 after one of his employees repossessed a refrigerator from a welfare mother with an infant, plunking her meat and milk on the kitchen table.

Yet abuses continue. Anthony Chapman, a Tyson Foods worker in Gadsden, Alabama, says that when he fell behind paying for a gold herringbone necklace, Rent-A-Center employee John Horton repeatedly showed up on his doorstep, brandishing two guns. The harassment climaxed, Mr. Chapman maintains, after he confessed that he had pawned the necklace. Mr. Horton promptly took Mr. Chapman's company-issue thermal uniform and a gold ring, forced him into the back of his van, and left him there during Mr. Horton's leisurely lunch break, Mr. Chapman says. He says he was then presented, in tears, to Mr. Keeling, the Rent-A-Center store manager at the time.

On several occasions after that, Mr. Chapman says, Mr. Horton ordered him to ride in the back of his van to deliver heavy items to customers. Feeling he had "done wrong and didn't want to make a fuss," Mr. Chapman complied. The intimidation stopped after Mr. Chapman managed to pay up, he says, adding: "This was the worst thing that ever happened to me in my life, period." One postscript: His gold ring, he says, was never returned.

Mr. Horton, who was fired from Rent-A-Center in July for unrelated reasons, declines comment. Mr. Keeling, the former store manager, confirms the account and says such harrowing scenarios are commonplace. Around Christmas in 1990, he says, he carted away the refrigerator of a diabetic customer after dumping her insulin on the floor.

'Couch Payments'

Yet another tactic in Rent-A-Center's repo repertoire is the "couch payment"—sexual favors exacted by employees in lieu of cash. Of 28 former store managers interviewed, six said the practice had occurred in their areas.

Some store employees have boasted that they "have gone out to the customers' home, had sex with them, and then repo-ed the merchandise anyway," says Ken Dube, who spent time at a number of outlets as a field auditor. He later became an accountant at headquarters until he was fired in December for reasons Rent-A-Center declines to divulge.

Mr. Gates acknowledges that abuses such as couch payments occurred in the past and "are probably going on today." There are simply "more control problems" in a business where much of the activity takes place out of the store, he says. But the company stresses that such abuses are "few and far between" and not "in any way condoned by Rent-A-Center."

Rent-A-Center says it is doing its best to clean up remaining problems. It set up a customer hot line that in July received some 2,300 calls, of which only 300 were complaints, the company says. In a given month, 99 percent of those complaints are resolved in the customer's favor, according to company officials. Some late payers say they have been allowed to skip payments. Rent-A-Center also sometimes rewrites rental agreements, stretching out the payment term to stave off a repossession.

But Rent-A-Center employees are sometimes willing to take the risk of getting caught, since the stakes are so high. In May at the annual meeting held at Bally's in Las Vegas, scores of managers clambered on stage to collect bonus checks at a festive final gala. As the champagne flowed, the store manager of the year was awarded a year's use of a new red Corvette, a trip to the Ritz Carlton in Maui and a bonus of $24,200. Rent-A-Center estimates that the average store manager currently earns a salary of $30,000 and more than 80 percent received bonuses last year.

As for Rent-A-Center's future, chances are it won't be quite so freewheeling. Aside from the lawsuits and the House bill, the Senate is drafting legislation. The Internal Revenue Service is also examining the rent-to-own industry. And Pennsylvania's attorney general has concluded that Rent-A-Center is violating a state law capping annual interest rates at 18 percent; it is asking the firm to give refunds. The state also is examining reports that Rent-A-Center engages in illegal collection practices, including threatening to break into late payers' homes.

Despite the proliferating challenges, Mr. Gates remains optimistic. He is hard at work on his latest pet project, "Rent-A-Center 2000." This store of the future, being tested in Kansas City, Kansas, features a play area for children, a "wall of fame" with photos of star customers and a "troubled times" program that enables renters to skip or defer payments temporarily.

Rent-A-Center is also branching out into new rental areas. One of its most successful has been jewelry; Rent-A-Center is now among the largest customers of Harry Winston, Inc., the famed jeweler to such clients as Imelda Marcos and the late Duchess of Windsor, which supplies lower-end baubles to the chain.

In its new ventures, Rent-A-Center will surely be able to count on its current customers, a loyal lot: Most feel they can't get quality goods any other way.

Nancy Thornley, an Ogden, Utah, housewife, for example, was diligently handing over about $261 a month in rental payments to Rent-A-Center in 1991 when she lost a leg to diabetes. Faced with a $1,000 bill for a prosthetic limb, she arranged to defer part of her rental tab, she says. But shortly after she returned home from the hospital, she was shocked when two store employees showed up without notice on a Saturday afternoon, accused her of being three months behind in payments and carted away all the goods, primarily basics such as a refrigerator and a couch.

"It was a total humiliation," she says. "All my neighbors were watching."

A year later, though, Ms. Thornley was back, having been inundated by Rent-A-Center letters and "We Want You Back" coupons. She was reluctant to return, she says. But "I needed the item," a microwave oven, and couldn't afford to buy it. Says Ms. Thornley: "I felt like there was nowhere else to go."

***

Pitching by the Script

Excerpts from Rent-A-Center's Sales and Service Manual dated February 1993

Closing

Closing is helping the customer to make up his/her mind. Many customers will be prepared to rent immediately after looking at merchandise. Attempt to close early in the sales track if you sense the customer wants to rent. Make at least 5 attempts to close with every customer. Closing methods include:

- Payment Close. "Will you be paying monthly, or is weekly more convenient?"
- Assumptive Close. "Let's get the order started."
- Delivery Close. "You can have that delivered by 4:00 p.m. today, or will 5:00 be more convenient?"
- Choice Close. "This comes in beige or brown. Which would you prefer?"
- Last Chance Close. "The sale ends tomorrow and I can't guarantee there will be any left if you wait... Shall we start the order?"
- Summary close. "Well... you agree it's an excellent price, you like the fabric, and we can deliver by 3:00 p.m. today. Do you want to fill out an order?"

Upselling

While using the sales track, be aware of and take opportunities to upsell the customer. Upselling means becoming aware of a customer need and satisfying it. Many times, a customer might not even be aware of his/her own needs. Opportunities to upsell include

- 7 piece suites instead of 5 piece furniture suites
- An electronic tune TV instead of a standard tune
- A remote control TV instead of one with standard or electronic tuning only
- A higher wattage stereo
- A larger capacity refrigerator, freezer, or washer/dryer

Whenever attempting to upsell, explain to the customer why the upscale merchandise is a better value and how it will satisfy their needs.

Part IX
Schools for Scandal:
Trade-School Scams

Rip-off trade schools have been around for a long time—trucking schools, beauty colleges and other programs that promise much but often deliver little. Media exposés began popping up in the 1970s—soon after the federal government sparked the industry's growth by allowing these for-profit operations into the student-loan program. Things got even worse in the 1980s when the Reagan administration slashed education fraud oversight.

Schools and banks have profited, while many students have been taken in by false dreams. Lilly Hunter tried to pull her four children off welfare and out of the public housing projects in Roanoke, Virginia. "Drive big trucks," the ad said. "Make big bucks." She says the school guaranteed her a job after she graduated. She enrolled and finished first in her class. But the job never materialized—and Hunter wound up $3,600 in debt and back on welfare. "This was me and my family's way out," she said. "I was proud of myself for doing something. And my kids was, too. But really all they got was their heart broke."

"The Perfect Job for You"

Banks make billions loaning students money for trade schools—
even when the schools turn out to be a scam.

Barry Yeoman,
Southern Exposure, **Fall 1993**

Juanita Shorter looked on as her classmates plunged used, contaminated needles into each other's arms. Their teacher stood by silently.

Shorter had come to Connecticut Academy, a private trade school in downtown Atlanta, to train as a medical assistant. The school's recruiter had promised her a free, government-funded education that would prepare her to work in a hospital or doctor's office.

Instead, she found a school where needle-sharing was common and waste disposal was cavalier at best. "We was fooling around with needles, blood," she says. "We could throw the blood in the garbage cans. We could discard urine anywhere. I wouldn't let them inject me with the same needle, though. I knew that needle was contaminated."

Despite her revulsion, Shorter stuck with the seven-month program. The school, after all, was accredited. And with the prospect of a good job to support her two children, "I wasn't ready to give up." So she sat up nights in her trailer memorizing medical terms until she cried. She bought colored markers and wrote the words over and over until she learned them. She even brought home clean needles to practice on her boyfriend.

It wasn't until she graduated that Shorter realized the training was useless. No hospital would hire graduates with Connecticut Academy diplomas. One doctor "told me he could not hire me with that," she recalls. "He said they'd throw him a malpractice suit quick."

During the past decade, thousands of poor and working-class Southerners like Shorter have been defrauded by private trade schools that lure them with promises of jobs—and then saddle them with big debts. In the process, the schools function as cash machines for big banks, enabling them to pocket billions of dollars in student loans guaranteed by the federal government.

Less than a month after Shorter graduated, a woman from First American Savings called her and ordered her to begin repaying more than $5,000 in student loans. "What loan?" Shorter replied. "I didn't make a loan. I filed for a grant."

The bank said otherwise. Without telling her what she was signing, Shorter learned, Connecticut Academy had tricked her into applying for a student loan.

Before long, the lender turned her account over to a collection agency, which called her four or five times a day, sometimes as late as 11:30 p.m., threatening to sue. Living on food stamps and $235 a month in federal aid, Shorter couldn't repay. The collection agent persisted. "She would ask me, do I have a car, do I own my house, how much furniture did I have?"

Shorter continues to look for work, without success. "To be honest, my future is at a standstill," she says. "I wanted to show my kids that you can always better yourself. But you look at my situation. What I'm showing them is: Your mama went out there and did the stupidest thing in her life. She listened to someone who was supposed to be trustworthy. She worked hard to get a diploma, and she can't even stick it up on the wall because it makes her so mad, because it's no good whatsoever."

Hole in the Wall

With public job training programs slashed and jobs hard to come by, private trade schools have become a big business. As of 1990, the last year for which the U.S. Department of Education has figures, more than 4,500 accredited for-profit trade schools enrolled 1.4 million students. The schools promised them careers as beauticians, bookkeepers, medical assistants, computer operators, truck drivers, secretaries, and security guards.

The schools take credit for training an entire class of workers. "If these schools were to come to a halt, so would

America," says Stephen Blair, president of the Career College Association, an industry trade group.

Whatever their value, the schools have flourished on government handouts: More than 80 percent of their students get federal grants or guaranteed loans. In fact, trade schools collect almost 20 percent of all federal student loans—some $2.5 billion in 1991 alone.

Some trade schools do offer solid training and good job prospects. But many have used shady salesmanship and outright fraud to exploit the dreams of the poor.

The trade school swindle is relatively simple. Across the South, hundreds of schools advertise on daytime television, and their recruiters comb poor neighborhoods and welfare lines looking for new students.

"Do you love money? The feel of it, the smell of it, the way it sounds when you crunch it up?" asks one TV commercial. "If green is your favorite color, we have a perfect job for you. Become a bank teller and get paid to work with money.... You'll be rolling in the dough before you know it."

Lured by promises of a free education and a guaranteed job, students come to the school, take a token admissions test, and sign some financial aid forms. It is only when they get to class that they realize it's a sham.

In Miami, a respiratory-therapy school was equipped with broken machines; students had to enter through a hole in the wall of an X-rated tape store. In Albany, Georgia, a school charged more than $4,000 to train students as low-wage nursing-home aides—while a nearby public school offered the same course for $20. In Florida, a chain of schools for travel agents spent more than half its budget on recruiters—and less than two percent on teachers and classroom materials.

Confronted by such scams, some students drop out. Others graduate, only to discover that their school has no job placement service. Many are hounded by banks and collection agencies to repay their student loans. They cannot get a job because their diplomas are worthless; they cannot go back to school because they have defaulted on one student loan and can't get another. The disasters start spiraling.

When Kathy Walbert graduated from Connecticut

Academy and found herself unemployable, she and her disabled husband needed money to eat. But with their wrecked credit, they couldn't take out a loan against the modest house they own in East Atlanta. So Walbert hocked her wedding ring and a pistol at a pawnshop, and now she pays $12.50 a month—at 150 percent annual interest—to keep them from being sold.

"We don't even have money to buy groceries with. We can't even afford nitty-gritty. We've got $3 in the bank," says Walbert. "I'll tell you the truth: I wish I never went to the school. It really messed up my life."

Phil Mebane attended a training session the school held for its recruiters. In an affidavit, Mebane said the director of admissions "made it clear that the school's sole purpose was to make money by obtaining federal financial aid funds. It appeared that the school's teachers were employed simply to keep the students entertained so that they would stay in school for at least six days—until the student loan check came in."

According to Mebane, the admissions officer "said that the school did not care if the students learned anything."

Michael Sykes, the director of the now-defunct Connecticut Academy, insists that he ran a legitimate school. The teachers, he said in a court deposition, "were dedicated to what they did and had backgrounds important to the fields."

Sykes acknowledges that health inspectors had cited the school for unsterile conditions and improper handling of medical waste. "It's possible," he said, "that someone got a little lax."

The Truck Man

Trade school officials like Sykes aren't the only ones who profit from the fraud. According to the Department of Education, banks make $1 billion a year processing student loans—earning a higher rate of return than what they make on auto loans, home mortgages, and government securities.

Typically, a school bundles up batches of loan applications and sends them to a lender. Since the government guarantees the loans, the bank has no incentive to check out a student's credit or a school's reputation. The lenders advance money to the school, confident they'll get their money back, no matter what.

Even when students get cheated, banks make money. Lenders accused of profiting from trade school fraud include Florida Federal Savings and Loan, Crestar Bank of Virginia, Wachovia Bank of North Carolina, and Charleston National Bank of West Virginia.

"It's very hard for a banker, operating at arm's length in making loans, to assess just how good or bad a particular academic program is," says David Hardesty, an attorney for the West Virginia Bankers Association.

For years, the federal government made at least nominal attempts to ferret out the swindlers. But when Ronald Reagan became president in 1981, he began his crusade to dismantle the Department of Education. Over the next six years, the number of government reviews of trade schools dropped from 1,058 to 372. At the same time, the amount of federal aid skyrocketed.

"It was like throwing money into an open field," says Brian Thompson, a spokesman for the Career College Association.

The abuses skyrocketed too. In Nashville, Tennessee, a beauty-school owner named Tommy Wayne Downs applied for—and received—$175,000 in loans for imaginary students. He got caught only when his secretary accidentally tipped off the federal government.

Downs began his career as a recruiter for a home-study course in truck driving. He was so eager to recruit students that he would take them to pawnshops to sell their belongings for tuition down payments.

"I focused my attention on welfare offices, unemployment lines, and housing projects, where I became so familiar that some of the residents referred to me as the 'truck man,'" he told a U.S. Senate panel. "My approach to a prospective student was that if he could breathe, scribble his name, had a driver's license, and was over 18 years of age, he was qualified."

"What you sell is basically one thing," Downs added. "You sell dreams. And so 99 percent of my sales were made in poor black areas."

Many schools began accepting students who couldn't

possibly finish the course work—but who could help rake in guaranteed loan money. In Durham, North Carolina, Rutledge College lured a mentally retarded man named Tilton Thompson away from a Goodwill Industries training program with promises of special tutoring and a guaranteed job. He received neither. Thompson got his loan canceled only after a Legal Services attorney threatened to sue.

Like many trade schools, Rutledge College was no fly-by-night operation. For years it was part of a nationwide chain of 27 schools owned by George Shinn, owner of the Charlotte Hornets pro basketball team and a major donor to Republican candidates like South Carolina Senator Ernest Hollings and former North Carolina Governor Jim Martin. Banks like Manufacturers Hanover Trust were pleased to do business with his trade schools—even though they boasted a student dropout rate of 20 percent every six weeks.

"It's a rip-off for poor people," Rutledge graduate Vivian Green told *The Charlotte Observer*. "It feeds poor people's dreams—people who want to do better."

"Fraud and Abuse"

Although trade school fraud occurs nationwide, widespread poverty in the South has made the region a particularly fertile territory for the scam artists. In Virginia this past May, the attorney general charged Commonwealth Educational Systems with encouraging students at five business schools to forge spouses' signatures on loan documents, falsifying records to collect loans from dropouts, inflating the credentials of instructors—even telling prospective students that the eight-year-old school was founded in 1889.

"Where the most vulnerable exist, that's where there seems to be the most ripoffs," says Jon Sheldon, an attorney with the National Consumer Law Center.

As early as 1985, the U.S. Government Accounting Office charged that two thirds of trade schools were lying to students—overstating job placement rates for graduates, for example, or offering "free scholarships" that did not reduce tuition.

It took Congress until 1990 to do anything about it. That year, more than 40 percent of all trade school students defaulted on their loans. "Usually it's the students who have not gotten an education who are most likely to default," says Darlene Graham, a North Carolina assistant attorney general. All told, unpaid loans cost taxpayers $2.9 billion last year—or 44 cents out of every dollar spent on federal student loans.

A Senate subcommittee chaired by Georgia Democrat Sam Nunn investigated and found "fraud and abuse at every level" of the student loan program—particularly among trade schools. In response, the Department of Education cut off aid to 828 schools with high default rates, forcing many to close. And Congress passed a law toughening accreditation standards and forgiving loans to some defrauded students.

Brian Thompson of the Career College Association insists the new measures have eliminated abuse by forcing the worst offenders to shut down. "Granted, there were abuses in the past," he says. "All of that has been changed. All of that has been corrected."

But while the feds can now cut off aid to outlaw schools, it may take years to shut them down. "That's a slow way of getting at fraud," says Sheldon of the National Consumer Law Center. "You need day-to-day policing." What's more, thousands of students still owe money for the worthless education they were sold before the new law took effect.

Landmark Case

Tim Tipton wanted to spend his life doing more than working in a tool-and-die shop. He saw his future in his hometown paper in West Virginia.

There, in an advertisement, Northeastern Business College promised to train students in computer-aided drafting. It seemed like a perfect career move: "I figured with my background, working with blueprints, I shouldn't be bad off."

But once he signed the papers for a $3,500 student loan, he learned the school didn't even have computers. "When we went in, they gave me shit that I could have bought for 30 or 40 bucks at any bookstore," he says. The only equipment was a "very basic manual drafting kit," and the textbooks were outdated. "Any kid in the eighth grade can get into any vo-tech school and get those books or better," he says.

Tipton tried to stick with the program. When he complained about the poor equipment, school officials claimed new machines were coming. It didn't take him long to figure out the computers would never arrive, he says, and three months after enrolling, Tipton dropped out. Soon after, Northeastern Business College closed down.

When Charleston National Bank started hounding Tipton, he contacted the Appalachian Research and Defense Fund, a legal-aid group based in Charleston. That's how he became the lead plaintiff in a landmark case involving trade schools. "A lot of people have a misconception of West Virginians being hill-billies," Tipton says. "I wasn't one of them. I knew right off I was defrauded, I was misled, I was fried."

Since the school had already closed, it couldn't be sued. So Tipton's attorney, Dan Hedges, took on some even more powerful institutions. He sued a slew of banks and S&Ls for ignoring the fraud while raking in profits. He charged the Department of Education with slacking off on inspections and allowing schools to regulate themselves. And he accused the Higher Education Assistance Foundation (HEAF), a private group that insures student loans, of collecting fees without supervising schools or banks.

"It's not just the ripoff artists," Hedges says, "it's the government that sanctions it."

The banks and their insurer contended they shouldn't be expected to check out the schools. "I am not about to defend certain of these schools. There may have been fraud going on. I don't know," says HEAF attorney Wendie Doyle. "The fact is, the borrower made the choice to go to the school. If we were to be subject every time a borrower is dissatisfied with his education, I don't think there'd be much of a loan industry."

But a federal court in West Virginia ruled that banks can be held liable for acting in partnership with fraudulent businesses. The suit was eventually settled out of court. Tipton and three of his classmates got their debts canceled, and Hedges plans to file suits on behalf of 100 other students from Northeastern Business College.

Profits vs. Training

Students in other states, including Virginia, Georgia, Texas, and Florida, have filed similar lawsuits. Juanita Shorter has become the lead plaintiff in a class-action suit involving former Connecticut Academy students.

LaRonda Barnes, the Atlanta Legal Aid attorney who filed the suit, hopes the spate of lawsuits will give pause to educational predators. But she knows that court cases alone won't end the scams as long as the loan system offers easy money instead of adult education.

"Once you put the profit element in there," Barnes says, "you're running the risk that people will be doing this only to make money."

Others agree. "It's a ridiculous system to take kids who are very unsophisticated about a lot of things and give them a sea of loan papers from people who pull them off a welfare line," says Jon Sheldon of the National Consumer Law Center. "Why is the federal government juicing this as a way of training people?"

The government has taken some steps to reform the system. In August, Congress passed a law that will take 60 percent of the student loan business out of the hands of banks—lending the money directly to students, without going through commercial lenders. In addition, the Department of Education now says banks can be held accountable for fraud committed by trade schools.

Sheldon and other consumer advocates say the government needs to go even farther by establishing uniform accreditation standards for trade schools and performing the type of surprise inspections that restaurants and other businesses routinely face. The government should also encourage real job training by contracting with businesses or non-profit groups to provide training in targeted fields where jobs will be available, supporting community colleges that hold classes in housing projects, and providing counseling to assist students in making the right career choices.

Without such community alternatives and tougher regulation, trade schools and the banks that finance them will continue to profit from fraud. "Were I released from prison tomorrow, I could go out and do the very same thing again," says Tommy Downs, the Nashville beauty-school operator serving time for fraud. "I mean, you are talking about the ability to steal unfathomable amounts of money."

Part X
The Politics of Rich and Poor
The Struggle over Corporate Profits
and Consumer Rip-Offs

Consumers are usually outgunned when they take on big corporations. This is especially true when it comes to lower-income and minority folks—the people who have the least clout in the political system. But some are fighting back: Well-organized consumers have won victories in Boston, Georgia, Alabama and other places. But their achievements have been modest so far, because the finance industry is a powerful foe. The nation's leading downscale lender, Associates Corp., has lobbied hard to head off legislation it believes would hurt its bottom line. In June of 1992, the Ford subsidiary moved decisively before Congress considered a proposal to forbid lenders from using the "Rule of 78s"—a mathematical trick tucked away in many finance-company contracts that penalizes borrowers who pay their loans off early. The rule overstates the amount due on early payoffs, giving the lender a generous bonus if a customer refinances the first loan in favor of a second one (a routine event at finance companies).

An inter-office memo from T.R. Slone, the head of Associates' U.S. operations, tersely described the effect of outlawing the Rule of 78s: "This would cost us millions of dollars." That memo and an accompanying one addressed to "All Consumer Branches" instructed employees to lobby Congress. "Have each employee individually call their majority and minority member(s) and *strongly* urge them to vote against the repeal." The repeal legislation eventually passed, but it included an exception that allows lenders to use the Rule of 78s on loans of 61 months or less. It was a major concession to Associates and the rest of the consumer-finance industry, which typically writes shorter-term loans than banks.

Little Relief for Consumers

Michael Hudson,
The Roanoke (Virginia) *Times*, **Dec. 12, 1994**

When it came to mortgage fraud, Virginia was out in front of the rest of the nation. In 1980, Bill Runnells saw the changes sweeping the lending industry—and he saw a chance to get rich. Runnells was an eighth grade dropout, an ex-Bible salesman, a loanshark, a pathological gambler, a shadowy man with a shaved head and dark glasses whose hero was Howard Hughes. As Virginia and other states began loosening regulations on mortgage lending, Runnells started a company in Virginia Beach called Landbank Equity Corp.

The company lent to homeowners who were already in debt, often desperately so. Runnells had worked at a finance company in the 1960s and had figured out a simple fact: People are willing to pay just about any price to borrow money in order to get their creditors off their backs.

About 10,000 families in Virginia, Maryland, South Carolina and Alabama fell victim to Landbank's sales pitch and astronomical fees. Some paid upfront fees and closing costs that equaled 50 percent of the money they actually borrowed. Hundreds lost their homes. It was a $200 million scheme that enlisted the help of dozens of respectable banks and savings and loans and the government-chartered Federal National Mortgage Association—and then made dupes out of those institutions too.

Runnells stayed in business five years, thanks largely to the Virginia General Assembly's loathing for regulations on industry. Legislation to limit fees that Landbank and other lenders charged died in committee in 1985. Sen. Peter Babalas—a Norfolk Democrat who had earned $66,000 in legal fees from Landbank—cast the deciding vote. A company voucher for $3,000 carried a notation: "This was one we agreed to pay after he stopped legislation in Richmond."

In the end, Babalas was censured by his Senate colleagues for accepting a bribe. Runnells, his wife Marika and other company executives went to prison for defrauding investors.

The General Assembly eventually voted to require licenses for mortgage companies and put limits on the upfront fees they could charge, but not on their annual interest rates.

Consumer advocates say protections for the most vulnerable borrowers are still weak—and that other companies have taken Landbank's place and are now profiting, more quietly, on the high-cost mortgage market.

These critics contend that state and federal laws don't do enough to protect these consumers from getting gouged on credit deals—whether it's mortgages, used-car loans or personal loans. There are no limits in Virginia on interest rates on mortgages and used-car loans, and the legislature appears poised to eliminate interest rate caps on all but the smallest personal loans from consumer-finance companies.

Finance industry officials and their supporters say stories like Landbank's are the exceptions. They say lenders that market to low- and moderate-income borrowers provide a valuable service to people who have no where else to turn for credit.

"I believe in the free enterprise system—I believe in competition," state Sen. Richard Holland, D-Windsor, a banker himself, said at a legislative hearing this fall. "The better-managed companies ... will charge different rates" and prices will come down.

Nationally, the growing number of lawsuits and government investigations over alleged lending abuses has prompted calls for reforms in Washington and a few other state capitals. In some cities and towns across the U.S., the "predatory lending" issue has energized neighborhood groups to take on some of the nation's biggest financial institutions.

One result has been recently signed federal legislation that puts some limits on high-rate mortgage lenders. It does not regulate the rates they charge, but it requires written warnings about the dangers of these loans and restricts contract terms that sometimes are used to fool unsuspecting borrowers.

For their part, leaders in the "non-bank" financial industry feel under siege from what they see as unfair attacks from consumer activists and the media.

Nancy Donavan, chairman of the American Financial Services Association, concedes "there have been some unscrupulous operators in our industry." But she says fraud is rare, and that the rates charged by the vast majority of lenders reflect the costs and risks they face.

"Forbidding us to charge appropriate rates would not help poor and middle-income people but dry up their sources of credit," she says. "As for fraud, there is no legislative system on earth that has ever prevented it or will ever prevent it."

Donovan says non-bank lenders must "mount a broad counterattack—to explain the special role we perform, to insist on our value to the economy, and to challenge the consumer groups' claims to represent the best interests of actual consumers."

***

"When the banks say 'No,' Miss Cash says 'Yes.'"

Through the persona of "Miss Cash," Bill Runnells and Landbank drew in borrowers who needed money fast. Once they were in the door, loan officers often misled them about fees and interest rates they would pay.

Two sisters from Salem, Virginia, paid $3,750 in upfront fees and closing costs to borrow $7,500.

A resident of nearby Hollins, Alice Mae Garrison, almost lost her home to foreclosure after paying 26 upfront "points" on a Landbank mortgage. But that finance charge wasn't reflected in the annual interest rate of 18 percent that the lender disclosed. Eventually the Virginia Supreme Court ruled Landbank was guilty of charging hidden interest and other illegal fees.

But Landbank grew quickly, fueled by the help of 40 legitimate S&Ls and banks that bought its mortgages after the ink was dry on the loan contracts—taking over the right to collect the monthly payments and in turn funneling down money that allowed Landbank to make still more loans.

Banks and S&Ls also fueled the growth of another high-interest mortgage lender, Richmond-based Freedlander Inc., which made 38,000 loans nationwide before it, too, went under. NCNB, the forerunner of Nationsbank, was one of the Freedlander's biggest bankrollers.

Top executives at both Freedlander and Landbank eventually were convicted of stealing from their investors and were sent to prison. Runnells—who led authorities on a two-year international manhunt before he was captured—was given a 40-year federal sentence.

Critics said the General Assembly had been too cozy with the likes of Landbank and moved too slowly to stop its practices. At least four top legislators had business dealings with Landbank.

Delegate George Heilig, D-Norfolk, headed a joint legislative committee studying abuses in the mortgage industry at the same time he was representing a businessman who was negotiating to buy Landbank. Heilig said there was no conflict of interest.

In 1987, the legislature voted to license second-mortgage companies and to cap the upfront fees they could charge at five percent. At the same time, the legislature also weakened penalties for lenders who get caught misleading borrowers about their fees and interest rates.

Most state lawmakers say they see no reason to increase regulations on mortgage lending.

On the federal level, the High Cost Mortgage Act was signed into law this fall. It defines a mortgage as "high-cost" if its interest rate is 10 percent above the rate on federal treasury bills, which are now approaching 7 percent.

For loans that meet this test, the law restricts the use of prepayment penalties and other fees. It also assigns greater legal responsibility to banks and other institutions that purchase fraud-tainted mortgages.

However, some of the original bill's tougher provisions were dropped after industry lobbying. David Rubinstein, who directs the Virginia Poverty Law Center, said the new law will help, but it won't wipe out mortgage abuses.

He said high-rate lending is not as rapacious as it was during Landbank's heyday. But "there are definitely still predatory practices. There are people out there who are desperate for money and aren't very sophisticated who can be convinced to take out loans that aren't in their best interests— and put their homes on the line."

***

When Virginia's House banking committee met in October to vote on a proposal to eliminate the interest cap on small consumer loans, the bill's opponents weren't optimistic.

Currently, consumer finance companies are limited in the rates they charge for small personal loans—which unlike mortgages, are not secured against real estate. The State Corporation Commission sets the rates much as it does for public utilities; currently, the maximum rates range between 24 percent to 33 percent, depending on the loan's size.

But a bill passed early this year by the Virginia Senate was designed to eliminate the cap on small loans and raise the maximum that finance companies could lend on such loans from $3,500 to $6,000.

To start the hearing, Sen. Richard Holland, the bill's sponsor, offered one change designed to make it more palatable to legislators concerned about stories of abuses in the industry. The industry would agree to a cap at higher level—36 percent—on loans from $1,500 on down, as long as there were no limits on loans above that amount.

There was a motion for an amendment and a second, and committee chairman Heilig asked for a vote.

Delegate Bernard Cohen, D-Alexandria, interrupted.

"Wouldn't it be appropriate," Cohen suggested, "to hear from the opponents" before taking any action?

"I'd like to act on this," Helig said. "We'll let the opponents come forward [afterward] and offer any amendments they have."

The committee approved the change on a voice vote.

From there, an industry spokesman squared off with consumer activists who were still unhappy with the bill.

Jeff Smith III, president of the Virginia Financial Services Association, argued that regulation was hurting the industry. Since 1978, the trade group said, the number of loan offices operated by finance companies statewide has dropped from 415 to 313. This has left 32 communities without a consumer finance company, Smith said.

"The system is broke and we need to try and repair it," Smith said. The bill would "produce a cure" both for consumers and lenders "so that borrowers who come to finance companies have a reasonable source of funds at a reasonable rate."

Smith argued that taking the cap off the interest rates would increase competition and drive rates down. For example, he said, deregulation of credit-card rates has increased their availability: "Last night when I got home I had three credit card solicitations in the mail."

"The experience out there is that the rates will drop," Smith said.

The legislation's opponents disagreed. When consumer finance rates were deregulated in South Carolina, rates shot up, in many cases above 40 percent and in some instances above 100 percent.

"If competition worked," Delegate Cohen said, "it would work with the existing law." If finance companies were going to charge less, he said, there's no reason why finance companies couldn't do that now: the current law has only a ceiling on rates, not a floor preventing them from charging lower, competitive prices.

If the bill passes, Cohen predicted, "you're gonna see triple-digit rates being charged to some unsuspecting folk." Jean Ann Fox, president of the Virginia Citizens Consumer Council, said competition doesn't work in the consumer finance market, because its customers are usually the least educated and have the least bargaining power.

She also disagreed with the argument that the consumer finance industry is on the ebb.

In Virginia, finance companies' small-loan receivables have grown at a rate slower than inflation—from just under $365 million in 1985 to $371 million last year. But receivables from finance companies' other lending—which includes home equity and auto loans—has exploded from $415 million to well over $1 billion.

And, critics say, the industry's profits are still extremely high.

Since 1982, consumer finance companies have done exceptionally well on the two most-accepted measures of profitability: They made a higher return on equity than state-chartered banks in every year but one. Over the same time, finance companies' return on assets has been more than double the returns earned by banks.

Their total profits on small loans have risen 53 percent in the past two years—even though the SCC lowered the maximum rates they could charge.

The industry's spokesman said those figures didn't prove anything. "If profits are so great," Smith said outside the hearing room, "why has there been a substantial decline in the number of companies doing business in Virginia?"

After the debate was over, Smith came up with one more compromise: The industry agreed to raise the amount that would carry the 36-percent cap from $1,500 to $2,500.

The committee voted 11-3 to send the bill on for action by the full House of Delegates early next year. Heilig abstained because of the legal work he performs for finance companies.

Consumer advocates said the bill would reduce the protections for disadvantaged borrowers, but they felt fortunate to keep at least some limits on loans up to $2,500.

"We had to work real hard to get even that," David Rubinstein said afterward. "We were definitely steamrolled in that hearing."

***

In their battle with lenders, advocates for lower-income consumers must contend with state legislators' long-standing ties to the lending industry. Many top legislators serve as closing attorneys for lenders, and banks and other lenders give generously to state election campaigns. George Heilig, who chairs the House banking committee, received more than $10,000 from the financial industry during his last election cycle.

Pro-regulation forces also run up hard against state officials' philosophical distaste for laws that put limits on business practices.

When the Landbank scandal first became public in 1985, the state's commissioner of financial institutions, Sidney Bailey, gave voice to this philosophy in explaining why he didn't see the need to pass regulations to protect victims of predatory lenders such as Landbank.

"There's probably enough law to protect most consumers," said Bailey, who remains the state's top lending regulator. "There will never be enough law to protect all consumers. I object strenuously to being told I have to wear my seat belt. I am overprotected these days when I try to get the top off an aspirin bottle."

At the recent small-loan hearing, Bailey suggested that it made little sense to regulate prices on consumer loans, because the state doesn't regulate the prices of milk, gasoline or other items that are much more necessary than credit.

Dow Chamberlain, director of the Virginia Interfaith Center on Public Policy, had another view. He told legislators that Biblical traditions support usury limits to protect the vulnerable. He said the state shouldn't pass laws that "enforce contracts which may be legal but—by any spiritual definition—are immoral."

People who are desperate "will sign anything," Chamberlain said.

The state attorney general has sued five check-cashing companies in Tidewater and Northern Virginia, accusing them of making unlicensed loans with annual interest rates that reached as high as 2,000 percent.

Before his Landbank empire came tumbling down, Bill Runnells gave a frank explanation of what drives the market for high-cost credit.

"When you're broke, you'll borrow money at any price. It's like buying tomatoes. Everybody's got a price."

Reforming High Finance

Efforts to stop predatory lending and clean up the
financial system are gaining support from
consumers across the nation.

Michael Hudson and Adam Feuerstein,
Southern Exposure, **Fall 1993**

It was a rare sight under the gold dome of the Georgia
state capitol, where white lawmakers and business lobbyists
are used to being in the majority. Last February, hundreds of
black citizens packed a committee room and choked the hallway outside. They came to support a bill to cap the huge interest rates that poor and minority homeowners pay on second
mortgages.

With millions of dollars in bank profits on the line, Loyce
Turner—chair of the Georgia Senate banking committee and a
banker himself—moved to squelch the uprising. Turner
warned the audience not to clap or shout support as the bill's
sponsor, State Senator David Scott, made his plea for the rate
caps. Turner added that because the meeting was not a public
hearing, the assembled citizens had no right to speak to the
committee. "We are not trying to railroad or stop anything,"
Turner said.

Scott didn't try to hide his anger. "If this committee isn't
going to represent the people, I don't want to serve on it," he
said. "This is a strong miscarriage of justice. If this room was
full of white people, this wouldn't happen. The banks run this
committee."

The committee put the bill aside, but continued pressure
from citizens and the media paid off. After Scott agreed to
raise the rate cap by three percentage points, the committee
passed the bill on to the full Senate, which approved it by a
vote of 44-11.

It seemed like a great victory for consumers. In the end,
however, the banks won. When a House panel—also chaired
by a banker—took up the bill, the pockets of its five members
had already been lined with nearly $8,000 in campaign contri-

butions from lenders. With industry lobbyists packing the meeting room, the subcommittee killed the rate-cap legislation. "They don't want this bill *whichever* way we write it," Scott lamented.

It's an old story in Georgia and in statehouses across the South, where consumers have won few victories over the past decade and a half. Consumer laws in the region remain weak and ineffective—thanks to the predominance of free-market-at-any-cost rhetoric, confusion at the grassroots, and generous campaign contributions from banks and other financial businesses.

The result is a patchwork system of state and federal regulations that effectively exempts low-income and working-class consumers from government protections that more affluent consumers take for granted when they enter a bank or S&L. Across the region, predatory lenders operate virtually unchecked. No Southern state except Georgia regulates fees charged by check-cashing outlets. All but two allow pawnshops to charge interest rates of 240 percent or more. Most put no limits—or extremely high ones—on the interest and fees charged by finance companies and second-mortgage lenders. And government regulators have only recently shown much interest in making banks obey fair-lending laws.

Jean Ann Fox, president of the Consumer Federation of America and its Virginia affiliate, says the message to disadvantaged consumers is simple: "You're on your own, and we're not going to protect you. We're putting our trust blindly in competition—even though competition doesn't work when consumers don't have a real choice."

Stop the Shark

But as the turnout for the Georgia hearings indicates, things are beginning to change. More and more, consumers who have been gouged and ripped off are pressuring their lawmakers to clean up the financial system.

In Atlanta, a grassroots group called Citizens for Fair Housing has sprung from experiences with Fleet Finance and other lenders that prowl the second-mortgage market. In nearby Augusta, a similar coalition, Citizens Addressing Public Service, has marched on Fleet headquarters wearing bright yellow t-shirts that say, "Stop the Fleet Loan Shark." Members of CAPS have taken the bus north to lobby Congress and the Federal Reserve Bank.

Union Neighborhood Assistance Corporation, an offshoot of a Boston hotel workers union, is coordinating a national grassroots campaign against Fleet and other predatory lenders. UNAC has set up a toll-free consumer hotline—1-800-96-SHARK—and has pressured corporations that own shares in Fleet to sell their stock.

Community-reinvestment advocates like ACORN—Association of Community Organizations for Reform Now—are stepping up the pressure on banks to lend money and provide services to low-income and minority neighborhoods. The second-mortgage scandal across the South has provided them with new ammunition in their fight against lending discrimination by bringing forward people who can attest, in a very personal way, to its effects.

Dorothy Thrasher, a 61-year-old homeowner in northwest Atlanta, told state legislators how two vinyl siding salesmen pressured her for weeks with an offer to make her home a low-cost demonstration model. She finally gave in, and ended up with an $18,000 home-repair loan at 23 percent interest. Fleet Finance purchased the loan and began collecting the monthly payments of $335, leaving Thrasher only $90 from her government pension check to buy food, utilities, and medicine.

"When I testified, I just told the truth about what those people had done to me," Thrasher says. "The whole place was filled with so many sad folks, most worse off than me. I felt like we was going to get some response, but I was disappointed. It looks like Fleet has too much control. They got the money, and all we got is our stories."

Money and Votes

Why weren't those stories enough to sway the legislature? An examination of campaign finance reports indicates why lawmakers remain deaf to the voices of disadvantaged consumers—and why legislation to protect consumers is so often subverted in Georgia and other Southern states.

The banking industry is a patron of most key members of

the Georgia legislature:

• The 10 members of the Senate banking committee received a total of more than $22,000 from the lending industry last year. On the House side, the 25 members of the banking panel—including those who killed the rate-cap bill—pocketed over $29,000 in contributions from the banking industry.

• Turner, chair of the Senate bank committee, has received nearly $7,000 from the banking industry since 1990, including $1,000 from NationsBank. The Charlotte-based banking giant has drawn criticism for its recent purchase of Chrysler First, a huge mortgage company accused of predatory lending against low-income borrowers.

• Senator Chuck Clay, the committee vice chair, took in more than $3,000 from banks last year, including $500 from NationsBank. He is also representing Fleet Finance in a class-action suit charging the company with racketeering and fraud.

• The Georgia Mortgage Bankers Association funneled more than $18,000 in campaign contributions to Georgia lawmakers last year through its Good Government Fund.

• Three key members of the House and Senate banking panels are bankers themselves. Turner chairs First Bank and Trust Co. of Valdosta and is a director of its holding company, Synovus Financial Corp.

Other Georgia politicians also enjoy close ties to the industry. Governor Zell Miller received $9,600 from Fleet's PAC during his 1990 campaign. Fleet said Miller gave a motivational speech at a company management meeting a few years ago.

With industry money in their pockets, legislators replaced the rate-cap bill sponsored by Senator Scott with one requiring licenses for mortgage brokers. Legislative leaders say licensing will stop "99 percent" of mortgage abuses. Consumer advocates say it's a minor reform designed to head off real regulation. Second-mortgage lenders can currently charge annual interest rates of 60 percent; Scott's bill would have capped interest at 11 points over the prime rate.

Guarding the Henhouse

Like other Southern legislatures, the Georgia assembly

has always been hostile to regulations on business. Culver Kidd, a Georgia slumlord and president of a string of small-loan companies, fought fiercely against business regulation during his 45 years as a state legislator. "He would let nothing come through that looked like consumer protection," recalls Donald Coleman, an Atlanta Legal Aid attorney.

Kidd also helped his silent business partner win appointment as a judge in Baldwin County, where he ruled on collection actions against their tenants and borrowers. Before Kidd was voted out of office last year, the powerful Democrat—known around the Capitol as the "Silver Fox"—sponsored a bill that would have discouraged his customers and other small borrowers from filing bankruptcy.

Despite Kidd's loss, good-old-boy politics and corporate power maintain a stranglehold in Georgia. Across the region, a number of trends over the past decade have left disadvantaged consumers even more vulnerable:

• Budget cuts have forced many consumer-protection agencies to curtail their already modest efforts. In Virginia, the state Office of Consumer Affairs has laid off workers and eliminated its toll-free hotline for citizen complaints. Reagan-era budget cuts and growing caseloads have also forced many Legal Aid programs—which provide legal advice to the poor—to cut back on their consumer efforts.

• Many newspapers and TV stations have given up hard-edged consumer reporting in deference to advertisers, and to owners who increasingly value profits over public service. In North Carolina, for example, the Raleigh *News and Observer* transferred its auto and real estate editor to the advertising department. The reason? Executive Editor Frank Daniels III says the paper does little real reporting on the car business because "it doesn't make much sense to piss off advertisers."

• Government cutbacks and increasing poverty in many communities have forced advocates for the poor to concentrate on providing for immediate needs like homeless shelters and food. In the midst of a lingering recession, the fight for better finance laws and long-term reforms has often taken a back seat.

The Reverend Minnie Davis, chair of the newly formed citizen coalition in Augusta, says that many people assume that financial reform has "been taken care of, somebody's handling it. They find out it's really not being taken care of—and we're really in a stew."

With consumer attention diverted over the past decade, many states passed "deregulation" bills that reduced protections for consumers—often with little or no opposition. In 1983, Georgia lawmakers opened the flood gates to second-mortgage abuses by eliminating a 16-percent interest cap. The proposal to kill the cap passed the House that year by a vote of 156-0. "The votes were lined up in favor of that bill long before the opposition even heard of it," former State Senator Todd Evans remembers.

Massive Resources

Such obvious pro-business maneuvers will be harder to pull off in the future, however. The statewide scandal over second mortgages has sparked a sense of sustained outrage among low-income consumers and their allies. Grassroots advocates, attorneys, government regulators, and Atlanta newspapers have joined forces to put heat on lenders who profit from the poor—and on the lawmakers who support them.

But citizens fighting for reform face an uphill battle against the massive resources of predatory lenders like Fleet Financial Group. The bank—the 14th-largest in the nation—has hired the Atlanta law firm of former U.S. attorney general Griffin Bell, who represents George Bush in the Iraqgate scandal. It set up a $30 million fund to repay borrowers who have been wronged, hoping to stave off criminal investigations in other states. It held a press conference with Atlanta Mayor Maynard Jackson to announce an $8 million donation to revive minority neighborhoods. And it has tried to shore up its image by joining with the National Consumer League, a respected non-profit group, to start a financial-education program for high school students.

Other lenders have tried different methods for ducking lawsuits and government investigations. After it was hit with millions of dollars in lawsuits, ITT Financial Services began having borrowers sign agreements requiring that most disputes be decided by a private arbitration firm called Equilaw.

Equilaw tells creditors like ITT that arbitration puts an end to "excessive jury verdicts." But a California judge has ruled that the arbitration program illegally denies borrowers the right to sue, and a Florida lawsuit says the arbitration clause is unfair because it imposes a $750 hearing fee on consumers and suggests they must travel to Minnesota for a hearing.

"Basically you can create a collection agency with ultimate powers if you call it an arbitration organization," says Gloria Einstein, a Legal Aid attorney in Jacksonville, Florida.

Consumer advocates have had some success in exposing abusive practices at Fleet and ITT. But things remain business as usual for most companies that profit from the poor. Even as the second-mortgage industry has come under siege in Georgia, small-loan companies in the state continue to operate under some of the worst lending laws in the nation.

With the help of sympathetic legislator/businessmen like Culver Kidd, the small-loan industry has blocked attempts to improve fair-lending laws. The industry PAC, Consumer Credit People for Responsible Government, tells members that campaign contributions are crucial to their profits, because the industry is "a creature of the General Assembly." Last year, the industry dished out more than $28,000 to state lawmakers.

Such influence-buying has paid off. Georgia law allows small-loan companies to collect stunning interest rates: from 123 percent on a $50 loan to 45 percent on a $1,000 loan.

Food at Christmas

Consumer advocates say changing the economic patterns that allow the poverty industry to thrive won't be easy. They call for a comprehensive range of steps to reform the system, citing the need to:

• educate consumers about their rights and create effective organizations to ensure that grassroots voices are heard at the local and state levels.

• pass immediate regulations to limit the usurious interest and fees charged by pawnshops, check cashers, finance companies, second-mortgage lenders, and used-car dealers.

- create a unified system of federal regulation that puts the entire financial industry under one set of standards, requiring all lenders to disclose financial transactions, end racial discrimination, and provide loans in poor neighborhoods.

- expand non-profit, consumer-based alternatives such as community credit unions and empower people to create their own economic development initiatives from the bottom up.

Ultimately, consumer advocates say, real reform depends on shifting the control of credit from huge corporations to local communities. Backed by current fair-lending laws governing mainstream banks, grassroots groups have already forced some commercial lenders to promise millions in loans for credit-starved neighborhoods. But so far, critics say, most pledges of community reinvestment are just so much public relations.

In Atlanta, Carrie Copeland has been trying for years to get downtown banks to open up to her fellow public housing residents. Copeland wants banks to lower the minimum balance they require for checking accounts—which run as high as $200—to $25.

"The banks are good at everything except banking," Copeland says. "Other things, helping us in the community, they're very good at that. They give food at Christmastime. They never turn us down on good things like that. But we want to go a step further. We want to save a little money."

Other activists are starting to make the connection between banking discrimination and predatory lending. In Augusta, CAPS has gone from raising hell about Fleet to pressuring local banks to lend money in redlined neighborhoods and appoint minorities and women to their boards of directors.

The group started early this year. Its first meeting drew 60 people. The next, more than 300. They marched on Fleet, on the state Capitol, and on Washington.

"We have so many people in this area who have been hurt by Fleet," says Davis, who chairs the group. "They're just hard-working people trying to make a living." But it took a while for them to get organized. Most thought they were all alone—that they had somehow brought their problems on themselves.

"They were ashamed at first, because nobody was saying anything," Davis says. "When other people start speaking out, they kinda overcome their shyness and say, 'That's happened to me, too. You need to do something to help these people.'"

Next year, when the Georgia assembly meets, CAPS will be there. So will Dorothy Thrasher and Citizens for Fair Housing in Atlanta. Working together, they will try again to overcome the financial power of the lending industry.

"I feel like one day some good will come out of it," Thrasher says. "You can't keep mistreating people and have the problem ignored forever. God doesn't let good people suffer and suffer without no justice."

Part XI
Conclusion

Conclusion

Michael Hudson

John Leak wheels his dark Ford van into a deserted parking lot along Candler Road outside Atlanta. A Colonial-style brick building, imposing but vacant, sits behind a sign that says "Available 377-6411." It's a former branch of Citizens and Southern National—a bank where Leak once worked and a pre-merger predecessor of NationsBank.

Something dark and furry scurries from a trash bin out back. "There's a rat," Leak says, braking the van under 5 mph. "See the rat coming out there?"

Leak shakes his head. Across southern DeKalb County—a burgeoning black suburb where Leak now serves as a funeral-home director and economic-development booster—there are plenty of buildings that have been abandoned by banks. This financial vacuum has been filled by different sorts of institutions. "You don't see a bank from South DeKalb Mall all the way to downtown," Leak says. "But you do see check-cashing places and pawnshops.... Pawnshops have become sort of a way of life for our community." A block up Candler Road from the empty bank is Cash America, a chain-owned, Wall Street-traded pawnshop that offers quick loans at interest rates as high as 240 percent. The pawnshop sits across the intersection of Candler and Glenwood from the DeKalb County Department of Economic Development, which itself is in a building that once housed an S&L. Cash America's no-credit-hassles loans represent what southern DeKalb's economy has largely come to—and where it's likely to go.

Across America, minority, low-income and blue-collar neighborhoods are starved of mainstream credit and services, thanks to a bewildering mix of hard economic realities, corporate merger mania, social disarray and educational failures, flawed government policies, enduring racial and class prejudices and simple greed. In metro Atlanta, predominately white neighborhoods average nine bank branches per 10,000 residents, *U.S. News & World-Report* found. Predominately minority neighborhoods average just 2.1 branches per 10,000 residents.

The story of America's poverty industry involves more than just individual consumers squeezed by higher prices or cheated by double-talking loan officers and trade-school recruiters. It's also about communities that are decaying because discrimination and exploitation have stifled economic growth. Neighborhoods go downhill when homeowners lose their homes to rip-off mortgage loans. High school dropouts snagged into debt by bogus trade schools lose what may be their last chance to develop marketable skills—the kind that are attractive to employers looking for new locations. As banks and department stores leave and are replaced by pawnshops and rent-to-own dealers, liquor stores move in too. Even if they keep their branches open, big merger-driven banks are less likely to care about these communities and make the kind of small business and mortgage loans that create jobs and wealth. "Access to capital is a lifeblood of any community," John Leak says. "Show me a community that doesn't have banks and I'll show you a community that doesn't have many jobs, that doesn't have many businesses, that doesn't have many people who enjoy a really fantastic lifestyle."

Father Richard Wise, a local Catholic priest, keeps a bit of his money in each of the handful of banks that serve the area. "I see what's going on: people want the traditional banking services." But the banks that do operate in these neighborhoods don't have enough lobby hours or tellers to meet the need. "When you go to a bank and 50 people are waiting in line—not because the tellers are slow, but because the bank is small—that says something." As a result, people end up going to check-cashing outlets and other costly merchants: "If I need to cash my check right away, you better believe I'll pay 50 cents if that's the only alternative. Muddy water is better than no water at all."

***

OBRON LINDSEY bought his house on St. Patrick Street in 1966. His was the first black family on the block. Within a year, he recalls, every white family had moved away and the street had become all black. Similar scenarios would soon play themselves out all over southern DeKalb County, just as they had inside Atlanta a few years before, prompting Mayor Ivan Allen to barricade streets to ward off unscrupulous real estate speculators. These "blockbusters" exploited—and often manufactured—the panic of white homeowners who feared racial change. They snapped up houses dirt-cheap and then sold them to new black homeowners at inflated prices financed at exorbitant interest rates.

Southern DeKalb's gentle rolling pastures, where cows and chickens once roamed, had given way to suburban homes for the growing white working and middle class after World War II. Within a single generation—from around 1945 to 1975—the white settlers had moved out and blue-collar and upwardly mobile families had turned the area into a mecca of black neighborhoods.

Doctors, lawyers, dentists and other well-to-do blacks have continued southern DeKalb's growth to the south and west. But the black neighborhoods closer to Atlanta that have been left behind are now poorer, with mostly blue-collar and low-income residents. Obron Lindsey, now in his 80s, says his neighborhood has "changed a good bit. Last year there was some shooting right down here."

Lindsey was born in 1914 into a family of tenant farmers in Jackson, Georgia. He came to Atlanta in 1955 and washed cars at Packard Motors. Then he drove a truck delivering appliances, with a junk-carting business on the side. Coming to Atlanta allowed him to achieve his dream of owning a home for himself, his wife and the nieces and nephews they raised as their own.

Illness and age have taken a toll. He can't work anymore and he and Mrs. Lindsey get less than $800 a month in Social Security. Of that, $159 a month goes to Fleet Finance, a subsidiary of New England's largest bank that has been accused of predatory lending in Georgia. Lindsey got a $1,000 refund from Fleet as part of the $120 million-plus it pledged in Georgia to settle class-action lawsuits and a state investigation. Lindsey's big problem now is the $451 a month he pays to NationsCredit, a former Chrysler Corp. subsidiary now owned by NationsBank.

In 1989, he borrowed $23,000 from Chrysler First Financial Services to pay off another equity loan. Six months later, he refinanced his loan with Chrysler First. "They sent me a letter and told me that they would finance it and give me some extra money. My wife had been in the hospital. And I said, 'I'll get this money and do some work on my house.'" He says he put in air-conditioning to make her more comfortable. He refinanced again four months later, getting $3,651 in cash and increasing his debt to nearly $32,000. His interest rate is 15.25 percent, nearly double the going rate for most home-owners. He's had trouble keeping up. His attorney has put him in Chapter 13 to try and protect his home. "It's such a mess," Lindsey says. "I can't tell whether I'm comin' or goin' sometimes."

**

WHAT CAN BE DONE to help consumers like Obron Lindsey, and to restore economic vigor to neighborhoods like his that are starving for affordable credit? Solving the problems of community decay—and the rapid advance of America's poverty industry—won't be easy. Almost all the trends point toward more growth for the fringe economy: Community banks are getting gobbled up by bigger ones .... bank account fees are skyrocketing and more families are going without checking accounts .... literacy and math skills vital to consumer decision-making are nose-diving .... Wall Street investment dollars are flowing rapidly into downscale lending .... consumer protection and legal aid for the poor continue to be favorite targets of government budget-cutters .... poverty rates, bankruptcies, foreclosures and other measures of economic hardship keep climbing. To fight these trends, advocates for the disadvantaged must work on many fronts: pushing litigation against dishonest businesses, improving consumer education and government consumer protection, and creating alternative, non-profit institutions that provide fair-priced financial services and real educational opportunities.

Legal Aid attorneys and private lawyers have been going after high-interest lenders and sham trade schools with increasing success since the early 1990s. The lawsuits have chased some out of business, and forced others to change their practices. In Alabama, juries have come back with huge verdicts against big lenders, including Mercury Finance ($50 million), Union Mortgage ($45 million) and Associates Financial Services ($34.5 million). Many of these verdicts have been reduced or settled out of court, and finance-industry spokespeople have taken to characterizing Alabama's court system as a "lawsuit lottery" where the odds are stacked against deep-pocketed corporations. But many of the lawsuits uncovered patterns of wrongdoing that cry out for punishment. "It's clear that some of these verdicts are just crazy," says Gene Marsh, a University of Alabama law professor and an expert on his state's consumer credit laws. "But they're the result of juries just being furious about some of the business practices in this state."

Even if they drive some poverty profiteers out, lawsuits alone won't make the problem go away. People need credit—and often buy into the notion that they need it even when they'd be better off without it. They need affordable alternatives—the kind that some advocates are already creating in many communities across the nation. These include an estimated 300 "community development credit unions" that serve low-income consumers. These non-profit, depositor-owned institutions offer credit and savings accounts to factory workers, elderly folks and welfare recipients at decent rates—without packing on insurance charges and other fees that many downscale lenders do. For hundreds of miles around Berea, Kentucky, Central Appalachian People's Federal Credit Union lends out nearly $2 million a year to poor and working-class borrowers. It has 1,700 individual members and almost 50 member organizations, such as schools, housing projects, even a plastics factory, that act as the credit union's branches.

One Central Appalachian member went to Kentucky Finance Co.—which is owned by a subsidiary of Ford Motor Co.—to borrow $500. At the finance company, he had to put up his car as collateral. Then the lender added in car insurance, credit insurance, an auto-club membership and its own fees, spiking his total loan up to nearly $800. At 36 percent interest, he would have had to pay back more than $1,000. He

escaped by refinancing with the credit union at 16 percent—
with free credit insurance and no collateral required.

Banks and S&Ls say poor people are bad risks—even as
they make the sort of high-flying loans that created the S&L
scandal. "They don't want to lend to poor people," says
Marcus Bordelon, a former banker who is now Central
Appalachian's manager. "But they certainly can get taken in
by promoters and real estate tycoons." Central Appalachian
shows you can provide financial services to these consumers
without going losing your shirt.

In the past, the credit union operated by mail and
through volunteers at its member organizations. But in the
spring of 1996 it plans to open its first free-standing branch, in
Jackson County, Kentucky. The county has a poverty rate of 38
percent, only one bank and, Bordelon says, "a bunch of
finance companies." Central Appalachian plans to fight hard
against high-interest lenders by opening branches in other
places too. "If we get a credit-union office in every county,"
Bordelon says, "we're going to put them out of business."

***

THE ONLY PROBLEM is there aren't enough institutions
like Central Appalachian, and they're tiny compared to banks
and employer-based credit unions. The average community
development credit union has about $2.5 million in assets,
compared to an average of nearly $20 million for all credit
unions. Put another way, Mercury Finance, the leading
financier for car buyers with bad credit, has more assets—
around $1 billion—than all community development credit
unions combined.

That's where banks have to come in. Banks and S&Ls—
which benefit from deposit insurance backed up by taxpayer
dollars—should be pushed to open more branches and make
more loans in disadvantaged neighborhoods, and offer low-
cost "lifeline" checking accounts to the poor. None of these
efforts have to be money losers, if they're tailored to these customers and modeled on the examples set by credit unions like
Central Applachian and by the handful of banks, such as
North Carolina's Wachovia, that aggressively invest in downscale neighborhoods. Bankers love to quote billion-dollar fig-

ures to prove their commitment to serving the disadvantaged, but many of the numbers are smoke and mirrors, and even those that are solid are dwarfed by the tens of millions of consumers out there who still need mainstream credit and services.

Banks shun low-income consumers of all races. But African Americans are more likely to be targets of credit "redlining," both because of subconscious biases and because race is often used as a marker for class. John Leak, the banker turned undertaker, doesn't believe it's a question of racism; it's one of economics and scale. "If you had a black-owned bank as big as NationsBank, its habits wouldn't be much different than NationsBank's are now." Big banks don't care about small accounts and modest home loans. "NationsBank is trying to sell people credit in Tokyo and Belgium. That's why they're backing the Olympics. They don't want my business."

Much of the problem is perception. The preponderance of pawnshops and liquor stores, for example, helps create a negative image of black neighborhoods. Driving past a "title pawn" broker—where you can pawn your car title in exchange for a loan—Leak points out businesses with weeds and trash out front and ugly storefronts. "You can't blame that on any bank," he says. He believes local governments can clean up the image problems that scare away banks and investment by providing better trash collection, increased police visibility and tighter zoning rules.

After he drives past a storefront called "X-Banker Check Cashing," Leak says there's obviously a demand for the services that pawnbrokers and check cashers offer. But they don't encourage savings, investment and forward-thinking financial planning the way banks do. "They don't create wealth for their customers."

"A bank will close a branch in a neighborhood," he continues. "Then a check casher will open up. The check cashing outlets do business with the same banks. The pawnshops do business with the same banks." The banks provide working capital to merchants that do business with "the same customer they couldn't do business with."

Blue collar people go to pawnshops "because the bank is

not welcoming to them. If the people in a community don't have a relationship with a bank, then they're going to feel intimidated and uncomfortable." To change this, he believes, banks must develop products and services to meet the needs of the working poor and lower middle class. Leak recalls that in his native North Carolina, credit unions used to offer loans with nine-month repayment schedules, to fit the needs of school teachers who didn't get paid in the summer.

Bankers don't realize the market they're missing. "The working poor have good character," he says. "They just don't have a lot of money." It used to be, lenders would ask, "Who are you and who are your people? Who's your momma and daddy and who's your pastor? Now that you're dealing with strangers, you let the computer do it." Instead of getting to know a community and its people, it's easier to say "Let's go to the line of least resistance," play the percentages and cater to the white middle class.

"That's not being racist in my view," Leak concludes. "What it is is not meeting the needs of the community."

***

FIGHTING FOR BETTER banking services and tougher consumer protection takes hard work—research, organizing, confrontation. Citizens have to let legislators and regulators know that they expect banks to serve all citizens fairly—and that they want reasonable consumer laws to rein in fraud and usury. Lately community activists have responded to the power of the finance industry by confronting it with in-your-face tactics. One day in the spring of 1994, a chartered bus pulled in front of a high-rise building in Washington, D.C., that is home to the American Financial Services Association, the trade group for consumer-finance companies. Inside the bus were 50 black men and women from Augusta, Georgia. They had ridden all night through the rain to the nation's capital to fight for the life of federal legislation aimed at regulating high-interest mortgage lenders. The bill had already been rewritten after intense lobbying by AFSA, and the industry was seeking to gut it further.

Earlier in the day, the Georgians had packed a Congressional hearing, filling the room with freedom songs.

Then they headed for AFSA's offices. Their leader, the Rev. Minnie Davis, demanded to talk to someone in charge. Jeff Tassey, a vice president, emerged.

"We came all the way from Georgia to expect this bill to go through," Davis said. "If the bill doesn't go through, we'll be back in ten times the numbers."

As the circle of people tightened around him, Tassey explained that his group believed the legislation went too far—that it would cut off legitimate credit to disadvantaged neighborhoods. "We're aware of those abuses that have occurred," he added. "I think we've dealt with them."

"Maybe you're trying to extinguish black people from having anything," James Brantley shot back. Like many in the room, Brantley had come to Washington because he had been bled by a costly loan from the notorious Fleet Finance. "It appears that y'all don't have any compassion in this place. And that's not gonna stand."

"I have to reject that—that a major a part of our members are as you describe," Tassey replied. "I can't sit here and say that all my members don't have compassion."

Bert Maxwell, 35, said he and the other protesters weren't talking about a few isolated horror stories. He said the pattern of fraud and price gouging "didn't haphazardly happen....It sprung up in the brain room. It left with a corporate stamp: Go out and steal."

When it was all over, the bill passed in a version weakened by corporate lobbying—but it was still a tougher law than what the finance industry would have liked.

***

IT'S WRONG to broadbrush every opponent of stronger regulations as a supporter of financial swindles. Many genuinely believe that unfettered competition serves the interests of disadvantaged consumers best. But reality is that the free market doesn't work well when consumers have few real choices and limited education. The less affluent often don't know their rights and don't know where to report rip-offs. A study by the Wisconsin attorney general's office, for example, estimated that just one in 100 people harassed by bill collectors ever complain to authorities.

It's not a burden on the free market to limit usury and crack down on clearly unfair tactics, such as "packing" credit insurance onto loan amounts or trapping customers into debt by enticing them to refinance again and again. Getting a loan or buying credit insurance is not the same as buying a gallon of milk; Comparison shopping is more complicated when it comes to credit. And going into debt brings with it the very real threat of losing your home, your car, your financial and mental well-being. It's not paternalistic to give downscale consumers a measure of protection when they're up against billion-dollar companies that benefit from immense marketing know-how, $200-an-hour legal help and big-dollar political clout.

In truth, a good number of merchants who cater to the poor and credit-damaged manage to make a respectable profit and yet offer decent prices and much-needed service to their customers. But fraud and manipulation are all too frequent—commonplace even—in the poverty industry. Trickery and greed aren't strangers to the rest of the American marketplace, of course, but the poverty industry targets the most vulnerable consumers. Often the attitude is they deserve what they get: They're poor, they're deadbeats, they brought it on themselves. That sort of thinking helps keep a whole subclass of Americans down, and ensures the nation will continue to be divided by race and class. It also makes it easier for financial predators to rationalize their own conduct. Many truly believe they're doing these folks a favor, treating them like a member of one big happy family—even as they charge them $1,000 for a $300 television, or sign them into debt at triple-digit interest rates.

In the end, there's also an unmistakable cynicism born of our "every-man-and-woman-for-themselves" economic creed. Some people simply have different standards of what's right and what's wrong, of what's fair: Promise them anything, they say, and buyer beware. "Get It Today—No Credit Hassles!" the ads promise. What's worse, the poverty industry frequently takes advantage of people when they're trying hardest to pull their families out of poverty: by buying a house to build up equity, buying a car to get to work, or going back to school to learn a trade. In his landmark 1963 book, *The Poor Pay More*, sociologist David Caplovitz wrote that the economy serving low-income and minority consumers "is in many respects a deviant one, in which unethical and illegal practices abound." A generation has passed, and little has changed. A few years ago in Chicago, a well-known chain of beauty schools falsely claimed in its advertisements that it had Spanish-speaking teachers, one of many deceptions it perpetrated upon its students. During the fraud lawsuit filed by ex-students, Legal Aid attorney Alan Alop confronted a top school official with these ads. The administrator admitted he'd been aware of them.

Q. "So then you did know that the D'Or Schools were promising Spanish teachers?"

A. "That's not a promise."

Q. "It's not a promise?"

A. "That is an advertisement."

Q. "Ah."

Appendices

Appendix I

Investigating the Poverty Industry in Your Hometown or State

Michael Hudson,
The IRE Journal, **Investigative Reporters & Editors,**
January/February 1995

The list of businesses and transactions that profit from consumers with lower incomes or bad credit is a long one. Here are a few examples, along with ideas about how to find out more about them in your community.

PREDATORY MORTGAGE LENDING is a serious problem in low-income and minority neighborhoods. Homeowners who are shunned by banks are targeted by finance and mortgage companies that charge huge fees and interest rates reaching 20 percent or more. Often these home loans are originated by shady tin men, brokers or mortgage companies. Big banks in turn profit from these practices by buying the loans from smaller lenders or by operating their own finance subsidiaries.

FORECLOSURE DOCTORS check official listings of people about to lose their homes, and then offer loans that will "save" the desperate owners' houses. Instead, they trick the homeowners into signing over their deeds or hook them into loans they have no hope of repaying.

TAX LIEN PURCHASERS take advantage of laws in some states that allow private businesses to "purchase" homeowners' overdue real estate tax bills. The homeowner has to pay back the tax purchaser—with interest. Many tax buyers use these transactions to induce the homeowners into taking out high-interest loans from them.

RENT-TO-OWN stores sell furniture, appliances and other household goods on time—for $9.95 a week, $21.99 a month, etc. Consumer advocates say rent-to-own stores charge markups that equal interest rates of 100, 200, even 300 percent. By doing shopping comparisons, you can document how a TV that sells for $300 or $400 at Sears costs as much as

$1,200 at a rent-to-own store.

PAWN SHOPS are fast becoming the banks for the bank-less. About half the states allow them to charge annual interest rates of 120 percent or more on pawn loans. Eleven of the 13 Southern states allow them to charge as much as 240 percent.

Don't be fooled by apples-and-oranges comparisons of loan rates: When a pawnshop says it charges 20 percent a month, that may not sound too high. But it does when you convert it into an annual rate. The way pawn loans are structured, you can simply take the monthly rate and multiply by 12. (With mortgages and other loans, you need to buy a business calculator that can figure the Annual Percentage Rate, which is the key to making a real comparison of loan rates).

CAR-TITLE PAWNS are a big scam in many states. Customers sign over title to their vehicles in exchange for loans. They keep driving their cars, but they often lose them because the interest rates are so high: up to 1,000 percent. One 66-year-old man in Atlanta signed over his car title for $300. The loan papers disclosed an interest rate of 24 percent—but it was actually 550 percent.

CHECK-CASHING OUTLETS are another fast-growing, Wall Street-financed type of "fringe bank." They generally charge 2 percent to as much as 20 percent of a check's value. A bankless family bringing home $16,500 a year will pay perhaps $300 a year in check-cashing and money order fees.

"PAYDAY" OR "POST-DATED" LOANS are an exorbitantly priced form of credit offered by some check-cashing outlets. They work like this: A customer will write a post-dated check for, say, $260. The check casher will give the customer $200, keep the $60 as its fee and agree not to cash the check until the customer's next payday, perhaps two weeks away. The real interest bite on these short-term loans can reach as high as 2,000 percent. Officials in Virginia, Kansas, Florida, Texas and other states have accused many check cashers of loan-sharking.

INSTANT REFUND TAX LOANS often carry interest rates exceeding 200 percent. Tax services, finance companies and check-cashing outlets give customers short-term advances against their income tax refunds. Some companies don't disclose the true annual interest rate, or even that it's really a loan.

CREDIT INSURANCE is a little-known type of insurance that finance companies, used car dealers and even banks use to jack up their profits. It's supposed to pay off a loan if borrowers lose their jobs, get sick or die. But consumer advocates say it's overpriced and virtually worthless to borrowers.

FINANCE COMPANIES charge interest rates of 30 percent or more for non-real estate loans of a few hundred or thousand dollars. With interest rates so high, consumer finance companies have a big incentive to pack on credit insurance to jack up the size of the loan. Consumer lenders also make lots of money by refinancing. About two-thirds of finance-company loans are to existing customers, either through refinancings or add-ons. Each time they refinance, they add new fees, more credit insurance, or assess exorbitant "pre-payment" penalties on the previous loan.

"SECOND-CHANCE" AUTO FINANCING is an area of wide abuse: Borrowers who can't get mainstream credit often are forced to buy credit insurance or worthless warranties and pay interest rates as high as 50 percent. Some used-car dealers run "churning" operations—they sell the car, collect the down payment and a few installments, then repossess it and repeat the process with somebody else.

COLLECTION AGENCIES and lenders' in-house collectors sometimes use intimidation and deception to harass people who've fallen behind on their credit payments. Some collectors will threaten debtors with jail or eviction, make sexual and racial remarks, or pose as lawyers or police officers. All this violates the federal Fair Debt Collection Practices Act.

TRADE SCHOOLS often rip off low-income people who are taken in by the promise of a government-financed education and the hope for a better-paying job. A 1985 U.S. General Accounting Office study charged that two-thirds of trade schools were lying to students by overstating job placement rates, for example, or by offering "scholarships" that did not reduce tuition.

***

To find out more about specific companies or patterns of

abuse in your hometown:

• Talk to local Legal Aid attorneys, private bankruptcy attorneys and non-profit agencies that do HUD-approved "mortgage-default" counseling. They are the people most likely to hear from consumers who have been ripped off.

• Call publicly traded companies and ask for their annual reports. Libraries also have a wealth of financial information and publications.

• Check civil court records for lawsuits involving these companies. For lenders, look at both cases filed by customers against the lender and at collection suits that the companies themselves file against their borrowers (these will give you the names and addresses of customers, and they sometimes include counter-allegations of illegal practices perpetrated by the lender).

• You can also use court and land records to establish the links between the local scam artists and bigger lenders: deeds of trust (which must be filed with the deed whenever there's a mortgage), mortgage assignments (which show when a lender has sold a homeowner's loan to another company) and Uniform Commercial Code filings (which can document business loans and thus show financial relationships between companies).

• To check local banks' lending records, contact the banks and ask for their federal examiner's latest Community Reinvestment Act report on them. The banks' community-reinvestment officers or the National Community Reinvestment Coalition (1875 Connecticut Avenue NW, Suite 1010, Washington DC 20009; 202-986-7898) can tell you where you can obtain local data from the federal Home Mortgage Disclosure Act, which documents mortgage lending patterns by race, income, gender and census tract.

Resources

American Association of Retired Persons

Consumer Affairs Section
601 E Street N.W.
Washington DC 20049
202-434-6030
Advocates for older consumers on housing, insurance, credit and other issues.

American Financial Services Association

919 18th Street N.W., Suite 300
Washington DC 20006
202-296-5544
Trade group for consumer-finance industry.

Association of Progressive Rental Organizations

9015 Mountain Ridge Drive, Suite 220
Austin TX 78759
512-794-0095
Trade group for the rent-to-own industry.

Association of Community Organizations for Reform Now

1024 Elysian Fields Avenue
New Orleans LA 70117
504-943-0044
Fights bank discrimination and works for home ownership by low- and moderate-income citizens.

Central Appalachian People's Federal Credit Union

P.O. Box 504
Berea, KY 40403
606-986-1651
Offers savings accounts and personal loans and conducts financial education seminars.

Bet Tzedek Legal Services—Home Equity Fraud Prevention Task Force

Manuel Duran, director
145 South Fairfax Avenue, Suite 200

Los Angeles CA 90036-2172
213-549-5852
Provides education and legal services for elderly homeowners in Los Angeles County. Publishes a newsletter,
Home Equity Fraud: Education/Prevention/Litigation

Citizens Addressing Public Service
The Reverend Minnie Davis, chairwoman
3534 Prince Road
Augusta GA 30906
706-796-1571
Local organization that combats predatory lending and
redlining in minority and low-income neighborhoods

City Limits Magazine
40 Prince Street
New York NY 10012
212-925-9820
Urban affairs journal that covers credit and banking
issues, poverty, slumlords, economic development.

Consumer Federation of America
1424 16th Street, N.W., Suite 604
Washington, DC 20036
202-387-6121
Conducts studies on credit insurance, access to banking
services and other areas of importance to low-income
consumers.

Consumer Action
116 New Montgomery St., Suite 233
San Francisco CA 94105
415-777-9648 or 800-999-7981
Statewide California education and advocacy group that
fights home-equity fraud and other consumer rip-offs.

Home Defense Program-Atlanta Legal Aid
William Brennan, director
340 W. Ponce de Leon, Suite 100
Decatur GA 30030
404-377-0701
Information clearinghouse for lawyers and journalists

investigating mortgage abuses.

National African-American Consumer Education Organization

Dorothy Garrick, Southern regional director
1613 Fairhaven Dr.
Columbia SC 29210
803-772-0204
Grass-roots group that is trying to develop local chapters throughout the nation.

National Community Reinvestment Coalition

1875 Connecticut Avenue NW
Suite 1010
Washington DC 20009
202-986-7898
Umbrella group for community groups that are pushing banks to offer loans and create branches in low-income and minority neighborhoods.

National Consumer Law Center

11 Beacon Street
Boston MA 02108
617-523-8010
Assists attorneys who represent low-income consumers.

National Federation of Community Development Credit Unions

120 Wall Street, 10th Floor
New York NY 10005-3902
212-809-1850
Provides technical help to low-income communities that want to maintain or start their own credit unions.

Neighborhood Assistance Corporation of America

321 Columbus Ave.
Boston MA 02116
617-267-1144
800-96-SHARK (Hotline for mortgage-abuse complaints)
National group that is organizing against predatory lenders.

Project Get Together

Steven Dow, executive director
2020 S. Maplewood
Tulsa OK 74112
918-835-2882
Anti-poverty agency that is fighting against high rates and abusive practices in Oklahoma's small-loan business.

U.S. Public Interest Research Group

215 Pennsylvania Ave. S.E.
Washington DC 20003
202-546-9707
Lobbies on consumer issues and conducts surveys on rent-to-own prices and access to banking services.

Virginia Citizens Consumer Council

Jean Ann Fox, president
7115 Leesburg Pike, Suite 215
Falls Church VA 22043
804-867-7523
A non-profit, membership group that lobbies for better laws on used-car sales, small loans, check cashing and other consumer transactions.

Washtenaw County Council on Aging

Terry Drent, executive director
505 Catherine
Ann Arbor, MI 48104
313-712-3625
Fights mortgage fraud against elderly homeowners.

Bibliography

David A. Aaker and George S. Day (editors), *Consumerism: Search for the Consumer Interest.* New York: The Free Press, 1971.

Alan R. Andreasen, *The Disadvantaged Consumer.* New York: The Free Press, 1975.

Ian Ayres, Fair Driving: Gender and Race Discrimination in Retail Car Negotiations. *Harvard Law Review*, February 1991.

Kevin Byers. *Fast Cash For Homeowners: A Study of Mortgage Lending by Consumer Finance Companies in the Richmond, Va. Metropolitan Area.* Richmond: Telamon Corp., 1994.

David Caplovitz. *The Poor Pay More: Consumer Practices of Low-Income Families.* New York: The Free Press, 1963.

John P. Caskey. *Fringe Banking: Check-Cashing Outlets, Pawnshops, and the Poor.* New York: Russell Sage Foundation, 1994.

Cathy Cloud and George Galster. "What Do We Know About Racial Discrimination in Mortgage Markets?" Washington, D.C.: National Fair Housing Alliance and The Urban Institute, Oct. 1992.

Allison Davis, Burleigh B. Gardner and Mary R. Gardner. *Deep South.* Los Angeles: The Center for Afro-American Studies, The University of California, Los Angeles, 1941, 1988.

Leonard Dowie Jr. *Mortgage on America: The real cost of real estate speculation.* New York: Praeger Publishers, 1974.

James Grant. *Money of the Mind: Borrowing and Lending in America from the Civil War to Michael Milken.* New York: Farrar Straus Giroux, 1992.

In The Marketplace: Consumerism in America. San Francisco: Canfield Press, 1972.

John Isbister. "The Lending Performance of Community Development Credit Unions." Center for Cooperatives, University of California, Davis, October 1992.

Arlene Modica Matthews. *Your Money, Your Self: Understanding and Improving Your Relationship to Cash and Credit.* New York: Simon & Schuster, 1991.

the Money Class. New York: Simon & Schuster, 1994.

Report of the National Advisory Commission on Civil Disorders. New York: Bantam Books, 1968.

David Sandford (editor). *Hot War on the Consumer.* New York: Pitman Publishing, 1969.

Gregory D. Squires (editor). *From Redlining to Reinvestment: Community Responses to Urban Disinvestment.* Philadelphia: Temple University Press, 1992.

Teresa A. Sullivan, Elizabeth Warren, Jay Lawrence Westbrook. *As We Forgive Our Debtors: Bankruptcy and Consumer Credit in America.* New York: Oxford University Press, 1989.

Surviving Debt: Counseling Families in Financial Trouble. Boston: National Consumer Law Center, 1992.

David Dante Trout. *The Thin Red Line: How the Poor Still Pay More.* San Francisco: West Coast Regional Office, Consumers Union, June 1993.

United States Senate, Committee on Banking, Housing and Urban Affairs. "Reverse Redlining: Problems In Home Equity Lending," Transcript of Hearings, February 17, 1993.

About the editor

Michael Hudson has written for the *Washington Post, The New York Times, National Law Journal, Utne Reader* and other publications. He began investigating the problems of disadvantaged consumers as an Alicia Patterson Fellow.

His reporting on this subject has won many honors, including a John Hancock Award for business reporting, a Sidney Hillman Award for social justice journalism, and an Investment Company Institute/American University Award for personal finance reporting. He has also appeared as a guest on National Public Radio's "Talk of the Nation" and "Fresh Air with Terry Gross."

Hudson has been a staff writer with the *Roanoke (Virginia) Times* since 1985.

About the contributors

Penny Loeb is a senior editor with *U.S. News & World-Report.* Warren Cohen is a domestic correspondent for the magazine. Constance Johnson, a former *U.S. News* researcher, is now a reporter with the *Wall Street Journal.*

Eric Rorer, a freelance journalist in San Francisco, recently completed a novel.

Mary Kane covers workplace issues for Newhouse News Service in Washington, DC.

Bill Minutaglio has been a columnist and feature writer with the *Dallas Morning News* since 1983.

Rita Henley Jensen, a former Alicia Patterson Fellow, writes a column for the *New York Times Syndicate* on women and the law.

Michael Selz is a staff reporter with the *Wall Street Journal* in New York City.

Andrew Bary is a senior editor with *Barron's* in New York City.

Martha Brannigan is a staff reporter in the *Wall Street Journal's* Atlanta bureau.

Kim Nauer is senior editor of *City Limits.* Andrew White

is the magazine's editor. Jesse Drucker is a staff writer with the *New York Observer*.

Jim Morris, a special projects reporter with the *Houston Chronicle*, wrote a series of stories in 1995 exposing landlords, employers and dentists who prey on immigrants and other disadvantaged Texans.

Alix M. Freedman is a senior writer with the *Wall Street Journal* based in New York City.

Barry Yeoman, associate editor with the Durham, NC, *Independent Weekly* and a former Michigan Journalism Fellow, won a National Magazine Award for public interest reporting in 1993.

Adam Feuerstein, a staff writer with the *San Francisco Business Times*, won a John Hancock Award for business/financial writing in 1994.

Editor's Acknowledgments

This book couldn't have made it into print without the help of a multitude. My apologies to those I leave out, but limitations of space and memory allow me to name only a few. Henry Woodward, who runs the Legal Aid clinic in my hometown of Roanoke, Virginia, was the first to suggest I investigate businesses that profit from the poor. Bill Nye, a sociologist at Hollins College, suggested this subject might make a worthwhile book. In my reporting, nobody gave me more help than Bill Brennan, Kevin Byers, Howard Rothbloom, Marty Leary and Lynn Poyner-Drysdale. Another font of information was John Caskey, a Swarthmore College economist who was the first researcher to fully explore the growth in the "fringe-bank" economy of pawnshops and check-cashing outlets.

Many others shared information, opinions, moral support or free lodging: Jonathan Kozol, Brett Williams, Margaret Engle, Pat Sturdevant, Jack Long, Ed O'Brien, David Ramp, Dorothy Garrick, the Rev. Minnie Davis, Anna Alvarez Boyd, Marcus Bordelon, Tom Methvin, Lance Gould, Alan Alop, Steven Dow, Terry Drent, John Leak, Madeline Houston, Mark Chavez, Michael O'Connor, Tom Schlesinger, Susannah Goodman, David Rubinstein, Jean Ann Fox, Irene Leech, Diana Hembree, Laurie Udesky, Dan Noyes, the Center for Investigative Reporting, Investigative Reporters and Editors, Doug Pardue, Katherine Reed, Dan Casey, Sean and Linda Reilly, Jeff Harralson, Allison and Pat Baskfield, Brad and Beth Krehbiel, Sandy Broughton, Walter and Janis Siemens, Jenny Labalme, Kathy Wilson. The list also includes: Eric Bates and Bob Hall at the Institute for Southern Studies and *Southern Exposure Magazine*; Sarah Pollock, Doug Foster and others at *Mother Jones Magazine*; Bill Warren, Rich Martin, Mary Bishop and many more at the *Roanoke Times*; Kathleen Keest, Gary Klein, Bob Hobbs, Will Ogburn and other attorneys at the National Consumer Law Center. I also drew on the work of many fellow journalists besides the ones whose work is reprinted here. They include Peter Canellos, Steve Bailey and others at the *Boston Globe*, Steve Kukolla, Eric Moskowitz, David Ress, Rob Wells, Paul Tosto, Adam Levy, and Monte

Paulsen. Many industry officials, store owners and stock analysts also generously shared their knowledge and points of
view.

I received much-appreciated financial aid from the Alicia
Patterson Foundation, the Dick Goldensohn Fund, the Fund
for Investigative Journalism and the Virginia Foundation for
the Humanities. Despite all this, this book may never have
seen the light of day had it not been for the determined ideal-
ism of Greg Bates and Common Courage Press. However, no
one deserves more credit than the people whose stories are
told in these pages: Deborah James, Annie Diggs, Wilma Jean
Henderson, Frank and Annie Ruth Bennett, Obron Lindsey,
Deborah Burnett and many more. Their fortitude and courage
in speaking out made all this possible, and they deserve
thanks for any good this book might produce. The blame for
mistakes, foggy analysis or misjudgments that find their way
onto these pages lies with me.

Finally and most importantly, I thank my mom, Gail
Hudson, and my son, Ben Hudson, for their unflinching love
and support.

—Michael Hudson
January 1996

Index